The World of Spirit
by P'shanta

Through the Trance Mediumship of Mrs Edith Thomson

THE GLASGOW ASSOCIATION OF SPIRITUALISTS

GAS PUBLISHING: scottcaroline191@gmail.com

To Mrs Edith Thomson, Harriet McIndoe and all the sitters in the Circle of the Open Door. Also, to the guides, controls and communicators in the Spirit World: and above all, to you, P'shanta, faithful guide.

CONTENTS

ACKNOWLEDGEMENT

Sheila Wright: granddaughter of Mrs Edith Thomson.

Thank you, Sheila, for your kindness in donating the letters, photographs, books and other records, giving the full story of your grandmother, Mrs Edith Thomson; and for allowing the Glasgow Association of Spiritualists to write this book in her honour.

INTRODUCTION

In 2022, during the Covid Lockdown, I received an email from a lady called Sheila Wright. She told me that her mother, Jenny, had died, and that it was Jenny's wish that documents and photographs relating to her mother, Mrs Edith Thomson, be gifted to the Glasgow Association of Spiritualists (GAS). GAS readily accepted them.

The records showed that Mrs Thomson had worked as a trance medium in Glasgow between 1934 and 1964. The notes were informative and gave a good account of her work at the Glasgow Association of Spiritualists (Holland Street then St Vincent Street) and the Glasgow Central Association of Spiritualists (Berkley Street), before, during and after the Second World War.

Some of the documents had been organised into draft booklets by one of the sitters in Mrs Thomson's Home Circle (Ms Harriet McIndoe), which was called the *Circle of the Open Door*. The drafts introduced the reader to P'shanta, Mrs Thomson's spirit guide, who had clearly provided good philosophical advice for Mrs Thomson and her sitters over a number of years.

Then there were the controls (Raymond, Julian, Rupert, David and Silver Pine), each one forming part of a group in the Spirit World. Their job was to protect P'shanta, and ensure that the mechanics of communication were adhered to, in order to create an environment that would render the process of communication between the Spirit World and physical world as smooth as possible.

By 1936, Mrs Thomson's work had already started to come to the notice of certain individuals, who were well connected with Spiritualism and Psychical Research. Sir Oliver Lodge (1851-1940), was one such individual. He was an eminent scientist (Doctor of Science and Professor of Mathematics) and member of the Royal Society. Sir Oliver had begun to study Psychical Research in the 1880s, but the subject had become personal when he had lost his son, Raymond (not to be confused with Raymond, the control), during the First World War.

Sir Oliver first visited Mrs Gladys Osborne Leonard (medium), and the evidence she provided during communications with his son, convinced both him and his wife, that there was, indeed, life after physical death. When Mrs Thomson also assisted him in this manner, a firm bond of friendship was formed. Sir Oliver was the author of many books. He also wrote the Foreword to *Letters from Sir Oliver Lodge* by J Arthur Hill.

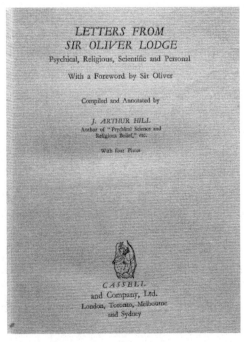

Sir Oliver signed Mrs Thomson's copy:

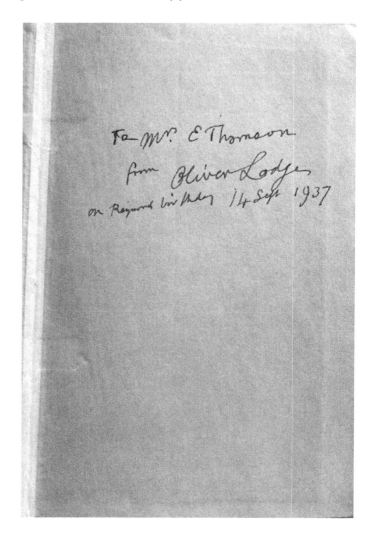

The message indicates that this would be on the birthday of Sir Oliver's son, Raymond.

Sir Oliver had already written a letter, the previous year, thanking Mrs Thomson for flowers she had sent to commemorate 'Raymond's Day'.

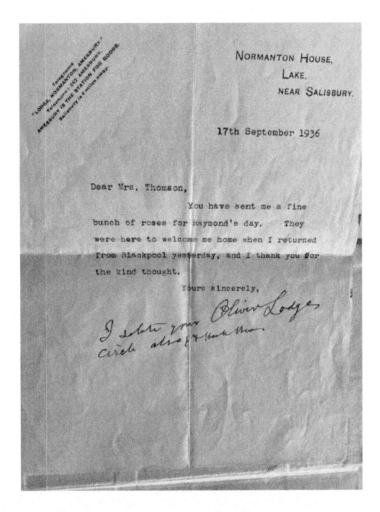

NORMANTON HOUSE,
LAKE,
NEAR SALISBURY.

17th September 1936

Dear Mrs. Thomson,

You have sent me a fine bunch of roses for Raymond's day. They were here to welcome me home when I returned from Blackpool yesterday, and I thank you for the kind thought.

Yours sincerely,

Oliver Lodge

I shall your circle also [...] Mrs Tho.

Mrs Thomson also formed a close bond with another eminent individual: Carl A Wickland. Wickland was a native of Sweden, who moved to the USA in 1881. In 1896, he married Anna, who was a medium, before going to Chicago to study medicine at Durham Medical College. He graduated in 1900, and following a period in private practice, turned his attention to psychiatry.

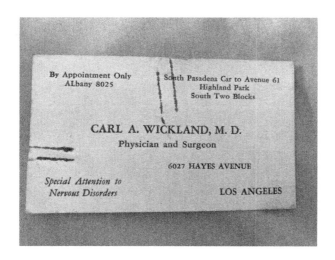

Wickland carried out extensive research into the interaction between the Spirit World and physical world, and determined that spirits might play a role in psychiatric problems and illness. His book *Thirty Years Among the Dead,* discusses his findings.

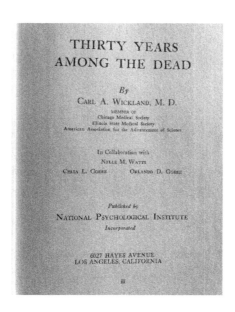

Mrs Thomson's copy of the book bears his signature and a message:

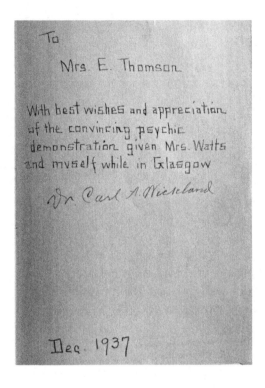

To

Mrs. E. Thomson

With best wishes and appreciation
of the convincing psychic
demonstration given Mrs. Watts
and myself while in Glasgow

Dr Carl A. Nickeland

Dec. 1937

Mrs Thomson's work was clearly well acknowledged by those in the know.

When the Second World War broke out in 1939, her work became invaluable. Thousands of soldiers and airmen, killed in action, were desperate to make contact with their loved ones, and through Mrs Thomson's integrity and diligence, she was able to assist them and their families by providing excellent evidence of survival.

This comforted those in the physical world and Spirit World, since it provided the knowledge that the 'deceased' were, in fact, still very much alive, and doing very well: thank you very much!

This book is a compilation of material taken from Harriet McIndoe's drafts and other notes. The original records and books are on display in the Museum at the Glasgow Association of Spiritualists.

Caroline A Scott
President
The Glasgow Association of Spiritualists
September, 2024

1

EARLY DEVELOPMENT

Paper submitted by Mrs Edith Thomson
at the International Congress of Spiritualists, Glasgow (1937)

Reactions to Trance

In this paper I shall try to describe my sensations immediately prior to trance. In doing so, it is impossible to avoid discussing the development of mediumship, since these sensations and reactions have varied with my development.

Before proceeding, I should like to distinguish between 'control' and 'communicator', as applied in my own mediumship. A 'control' is a member of an organised band of spirits, who work under the guidance and instruction of a leader, who is the guide, and who transmits the communicator's message.

The first time I experienced trance was in the presence of two other people. I yawned a great deal and experienced difficulty in breathing. My eyes became heavy, until it was impossible to keep them open any longer. The state was similar to the precursory one of ordinary sleep, except for the abnormal breathing, which was very much deeper, and somewhat laboured. I was unaware of the presence of any spirit personality. On awakening, I felt emotionally moved, rather ecstatic, eventually giving way to a flood of tears.

After this initiation, I went into trance once, occasionally twice, a week. Both sitters were entirely ignorant of any necessary 'conditions', and had no knowledge of what to do in an emergency. One sitter believed that discarnate spirits could communicate, but had no experience of them doing so, the other was decidedly sceptical. I, myself, was amusedly sceptical, though interested in the various communications reported to me, and willing to undergo the experience as opportunity offered. Such were the conditions under which were laid the foundations of my mediumship.

After perhaps three months, a sudden change occurred. A feeling of nausea attacked me, accompanied by rapid palpitation. Because of that unpleasantness, I tried to resist the drowsiness overtaking me, and for the first time, became aware very vaguely of somehow being forced against my will to give way to it. The first control, as defined above, had made his appearance.

Thenceforward, I found that my brain was increasingly active after sitting. I could not sleep easily at night, although feeling very sleepy during the day. I experienced very real pains in various parts of my body, and consulted a doctor. He eventually lost patience with me when he found my pains did not yield to his medicines, and that he was compelled to listen at each visit to fresh symptoms for which he could assign no reason.

This upset me greatly. I wondered if I had become hypochondriac. All at once I realised that my illness must be caused by my going into trance, and decided to stop, but was dissuaded by my two sitters who promised to consult the control. He declared that it was a phase which would pass, as their power to protect me from too-pressing communicators increased.

As promised, the reactions did grow less acute, although they did not entirely vanish. I found also that I could, myself, lessen the nausea and mental disturbances by refraining, for some hours before the sitting, from food and from contacts with people. It was also advisable, to avoid fatigue, mental and physical, and this involved a serious curtailment of my activities. I have since found these precautionary measures are essential to the success of my psychic work.

At this juncture, I decided it would be wise to become associated with people who had some knowledge of séance conditions, and I, with one sitter, joined a group of about twelve people. They varied as regards age, physical fitness, and intelligence, but they had been sitting together harmoniously for some years. Unfortunately, my control and the sitters were at cross purposes regarding the conditions necessary for a developing medium, and all the disagreeable reactions returned, greatly increased.

Along with these, came also reactions undoubtedly due to the sitters. For example, I was left with the taste of tobacco, obviously from smokers among the sitters, and I myself do not smoke. I also took on temporarily the aches and pains from which any sitter might be suffering. To my way of thinking, my mediumship did not improve during this period, but became muddled in character.

Eventually this circle disbanded, and I was fortunate enough to meet the group with whom I now sit. About the same time, it was evident that a band of spirits had gradually been forming to work with me, and there I was introduced to the guide, P'shanta, who has constantly been with me since. It is from this time that I date the more interesting phase of my observations, and the lessening of disturbing sensations.

Here it would be as well to state the different circumstances under which I now experience trance:

1. My home circle, for developing purposes only.
2. Circles for communication.
3. Platform work, consisting of trance speaking and communication.

I shall first describe the reactions which are common to these three types of work, and then those peculiar to each.

My entry into trance is invariably both easy and swift. My normal consciousness seems enlarged. I feel free and light, as though functioning in space, unaware of my body. Usually, I hear remarks by my controls, instructions from the guide, replies from others. This transition period is very brief. Gradually all consciousness disappears and I recollect nothing more until again I hear the words of the controls as I leave trance.

Thereafter, my mind is confused for a few seconds. My memory does not appear to function during a period lasting for anything up to an hour after trance. I am unable to recall it later. After trance, I experience a period of exhilaration, which, at the end of perhaps an hour, suddenly disappears, leaving me exhausted. Any pain from which I am myself suffering vanishes during trance, but returns when exhilaration ceases.

I have no sense of the passage of time during trance, except after a particularly long circle, when exhaustion tells me it has been longer than usual. I have tried by willing it beforehand to limit the time of a circle, but always without success.

I find that trance in too strong a light causes an ache in the centre of the forehead. I am invariably thirsty after trance, although in the early stages of my development, it was hunger I experienced. The reactions peculiar to circles are as follows.

On leaving trance, the mental confusion, although still lasting only a few seconds, is greater than after platform work; my surroundings appear unfamiliar; there is a feeling of wide space about me as though I were not within walls; I usually feel as if I had wakened suddenly from a deep sleep; my mind is confused and seems unwilling to resume normal activity; I frequently ask where I am. Within a few seconds, however, I am normal, with the exception of the non-functioning of my memory already referred to.

When a circle has been satisfactory, I feel very happy. When it has been difficult, I am disappointed. I assume that these emotions reach me from the communicators, who are either satisfied or disappointed in their efforts to reach their friends. In the case of a very difficult sitting, I do not experience the intervening period of exhilaration, but feel exhausted at the close of the sitting.

Trance for platform work seems to fall into a slightly different category. Frequently, I am aware of what is being said, yet speech is quite automatic. I can listen critically, yet can in no way interfere with what is said. This consciousness sometimes alternates with periods of complete unconsciousness, the changes being not sudden but gradual, resembling the ebb and flow of a tide. This experience of hearing what is said is commonest while demonstrating (that is, giving evidential communication from a public platform), but occasionally it occurs during trance addresses.

Conditions vary with the different controls who are working. For example, during the day on which I am going to give a trance address, one control will give me no idea of what he intends to speak on, while another allows ideas to penetrate, although in chaotic form.

When I first began platform work, I experienced a new phase of reaction. I was frequently unable to sleep because of the repetition of what I supposed were the messages given while in trance. When I eventually fell asleep, these continued as dreams, sometimes assuming the proportions of nightmares. This phase happily did not last long.

The home circle again brings us to quite a different set of conditions. It is the centre of my mediumship, and from it all variations spring. It is here that new controls become known to us, with their individual characteristics. The sensation and reactions which I experience differ with each one. After trance I always know if any new control has been introduced by an aching at the back of my head. If an experienced control has been absent for a time, the same condition appears on his return.

When certain new controls are operating, it has been observed that they are very sensitive to noise, even objecting to the pencil of the note taker, or the ticking of a clock, and hearing the ordinary tones of the sitters as shouts. The turning of a page or a slight cough can cause them to lose control. This phase does not usually last after the second experience of controlling.

In conclusion, let me state that in spite of all the difficulties I experience, I find the mental stimulus gained ample compensation. I have developed a mental clarity and decisiveness which I attribute to the different personalities surrounding me. I have been aware of subtle educative processes which cannot actually be defined.

Before my development, I had got to the stage of being mentally at a loose end. There seemed to be no purpose in anything. This mental state affected my health. Now I have regained a strong mental interest in most things, and am undoubtedly better physically.

2

NOTES BY HARRIET MCINDOE

A sitter in Mrs Thomson's Circle of the Open Door

Mrs Edith Thomson was a medium who worked in Glasgow between 1934 and 1964. Her mediumship was fostered and developed in her home circle, which was set up in 1932. I was a member of the circle for many years. We were a small group, which met in her home at the same hour each week. Notes were taken. They were in long hand, sometimes written in darkness, more often in subdued light. There was only one note taker, but the notes were expanded the next day, and doubtful points checked with the other sitters the following week.

The number of sitters varied over the years, but was seldom more than seven. Regularity of attendance and punctuality were enjoined on us, and we were asked to make certain preparations on the day of the circle, such as bathing, relaxing and refraining from drinking alcohol or smoking. One sitter was recognised as circle leader and acted as spokesman to the guide and controls.

We were asked to rid ourselves of any particular ideas we might have of the type of phenomenon which might appear, either on a particular night, or in the long term. An attitude of relaxed expectancy was desired. Music, singing and conversation were all welcome while we awaited the signs of the presence of the controls. These helped to focus together the minds of the sitters.

The purpose of the home circle was not to benefit the sitters, but to develop and strengthen the mediumship. The group of controls referred to it as 'our night', and as a laboratory in which they experimented with different methods, took steps to strengthen certain facets of the mediumship, and saw that all was in order. Evidence might be given to sitters, but that would be incidental perhaps to an experiment in a new way of presenting evidence.

There could be discussion between controls and sitters, which might be illuminating as well as interesting, but its purpose would be to give practice to members of the group (controls) in expressing ideas clearly through the mind of the medium. Towards the end of the evening there was usually a period of light-hearted conversation and repartee. The chief purpose of this was to lighten the atmosphere so that the medium came out of trance happy and secure. Another purpose served was keeping alive the interest of the sitters. Boredom had to be avoided.

The room we met in had to be comfortable and warm. Generally, we sat with a subdued light, but for certain experiments, darkness was necessary. The conditions varied in accordance with instructions given by the controls.

It is not easy to give a general idea of the happenings in the home circle. There was no such thing as a 'typical' evening, since no two were alike. There was, however, a pattern. During the first hour we were often quite unaware of any spirit activity. We passed the time in talking, singing or listening to gramophone records until the controls were ready to speak. Mrs Thomson sometimes saw lights or forms, or heard words which the sitters did not. At times, some sitters would hear or see those while others did not. Sometimes the medium would be entranced from the start of the sitting; at others she would remain conscious during the first period.

The sitters had to remain alert. There was usually a period of talk between the controls and the sitters. Problems concerning Mrs Thomson's work would be discussed and there was often general conversation on everyday events. Politics, new books, theatrical productions, exhibitions of paintings: the controls were interested in all of these, and showed knowledge of them. Almost invariably the circle closed on a light happy note.

Much of the time of the home circle was devoted to the perfecting of trance speaking and evidential communication. Indeed, by 1935, when the extant notes began, speech by the controls was fluent and accurate, and evidence was convincing. Mrs Thomson was noted for the highly personal traits shown by many of the communicators. Mannerisms, idioms and gestures often convinced us of the presence of our spirit friends quite as much as did the words actually spoken through the medium.

Those of us who sat regularly with Mrs Thomson, realised that her guide, P'shanta, was always present at the sittings, and that working with him, were controls: spirits whose function was to protect communicators and make it easy for them to speak to sitters. Generally, we had a desire to learn from P'shanta and the controls, and in 1940 a circle was formed for that purpose.

The members met regularly simply to listen to and talk with P'shanta and the controls. But the group of controls was not always static, and when a member was brought to the controlling point for the first time, he had to undergo a sort of initiation, proving that while in control of the medium, he could think clearly and express his thoughts audibly and coherently.

At this time, Mrs Thomson also gave 'trance addresses' in which one of the controls spoke to a public audience. Trance addresses were sometimes taken in shorthand. After 1945, we experimented with tapes, but at that time, the switching on and off of these was audible and proved disturbing to trance. Some records of talks and sittings were, however, obtained on tape.

Since terms in Spiritualist and psychic literature are not always used in the same sense, it is worth defining some words as they were used by Mrs Thomson's controls:

Medium

This is a person who is born with strong psychic powers which have been developed for the purpose of providing a channel for communication between the living and the dead.

Guide

This is a spirit who is in charge of a particular medium, and of the work done by that medium.

Controls

These are spirits who work under the leadership of the guide. They assist communicators and guard against intrusion. The controls associated with Mrs Thomson were known collectively as the group.

Communicators

These are spirits who speak to friends on earth. The latter are generally referred to as sitters.

Home/Developing Circle

This is a group of people who meet regularly for the development of the medium.

Finally, imperfect as the notes might be, I believe the information they contain is unique.

Not only do they show something of the development and work of one medium over a long period of years, but they also give glimpses of the work of the guide and controls, their methods, the difficulties they had to overcome, and the infinite patience they had to exercise over the years to produce good mediumship.

3

P'SHANTA

Ode to P'shanta by the sitters

We meet to honour thee!
Hast thou not taught us,
Blessed and guided patiently,
Cheered not chided us?
We hold thy honour high.
Truth is thy shield, a rock
Of integrity impregnable.
Woven is thy gown
With the soft sheen of stars
Lighting the purple night.
Thy fragrance doth cover us;
Garbed in soft purple splendidly
Bless and protect us.
Strong we shall be, courageous,
With right to defend us.
Take this our gift,
Love and its tokens flowers,
And our hearts,
O noble P'shanta, O gracious thou!

P'shanta's Reply

In the way of my people, I accept your tribute. I am highly honoured and accept it with the dignity it deserves. May I ever seek to find the true endurance to comfort and bless, to dry the tear, to put heart into the tired, and give courage to the timid. May we gather forces and lend our light as a flame to lighten the corner of the earth in which we find our abiding.

As thou hast sought to honour me, so do I return to honour thee and speak with gratitude of the love that enwrappeth me, the steadfastness and the endurance, the kindliness and soft humour, the gentleness and willingness to aid and protect me. The bond of brotherhood is of very precious worth and thou hast earned the reward of sure knowledge that, come what may, naught shall separate us, and though the swift waters run and the tides do follow us, closer, closer shall we be, and love abiding shall follow us.

To you, in flesh, I send my love and pray your hearts may never weary, but if in true attempt to establish my school thou endureth awhile, O patient be, and watch for the light that shall steal like the waking sun till it shines most gloriously; and to those who are my true and tried initiates, to you I gladly give the key to my full abiding. There are treasures, but thou must seek, and finding, keep in safe and sacred keeping. Love where thou canst and spread true peace abroad. Let not discord disturb, nor trying people wrest from thee the wroth of word. Schooled thou art and truly tried, tall in stature and clear in mind. Fair are thy lines and wisely chosen, and blest am I thus to have spoken.

Let us now pledge in solemnness and truth and unison our will, our word: 'We serve.'

4

THE WORLD OF SPIRIT

I believe that when I wake
Earth shall be green again.
Gone are the scorching fires
And burning glow of death.
I shall be free to wander far and wide
And light upon the hill there set so fair,
And look the valley o'er
The peaceful meadow and the church there nestling.
Sweet hour, what joy! What peace! And bliss so rare
That I would risk the crevasse there to gain it.
Where is thy rod and staff to comfort me?
Lo, in this abiding peace
I shall live and have my habitat.
Return, O Life, and quicken me
That I may spring from rock to rock
And scale the heights and drink the glad spring in,
That all my veins shall flow with blood again.
See there a high tower, shining and bright,
The citadel no doubt of many a dream.
O Weariness, oppress not my brain,
For I must faster go to yonder edge
And lay me down there quietly
To waken yet again,
And find the world is green once more.

This poem was recited during trance mediumship. The words came from a young soldier, killed in battle on 28 March 1944. However, it was P'shanta, Mrs Thomson's guide, who gave a detailed insight into the Spirit World.

P'shanta talks about life in the Spirit World

You wonder about the condition of people who have left the physical world. We who live in the Spirit World tell you the two worlds are one, intercepting each other; that we have the sun, rivers, trees, and so on, but that must seem fantastic to you. Experiences are difficult to convey to those who have not had similar ones, and to imagine our world as a replica of yours, is beyond the imagination of most people.

All descriptions of the Spirit World are hampered by the fact that earth language and imagery must be employed to portray it. Descriptions of the World of Spirit must be, to a certain extent, inaccurate.

The term 'Spirit World' itself suggests limited dimensions, but it is a place where people dwell without the limitations of the three dimensions. Earth itself is not wholly governed by these. You have the ability to go beyond them, but to do so, you must study psychic laws. The World of Spirit intermingles with, yet is beyond, the confines of the earth. In a different environment we can move with freedom through space and matter and other barricades.

We tell you we have bodies like yours. That is true, yet untrue. My body is a replica of the old one, but it is composed of different constituents. It is lighter than air, yet with a certain gravitation, so our point of gravitation must be different from yours. Ours is within us, not without, as on earth. We have power to draw to ourselves what we want.

In our world, as in yours, there are different strata of society, but for different reasons. Money and position mean nothing to us. Honour, truth, valour, above all service, are the insignia by which people are known. Those who would be great must become humblest in the pursuit of service to men on earth, as well as to their fellows in Spirit. Universal service is the law which controls us.

Life here tends towards simplicity. Possessions don't matter. What you covet can be yours. If it is something which does you no honour, you will find its emptiness more quickly than you would on earth.

When some poor person comes here, it's a delight to us to provide him with a magnificent house and furniture and grand clothes. For as long as he wants them, they are there. Then they disappear, and something real takes their place. As you grasp at the shadow, you learn to know the substance and to hold it always.

P'shanta talks about dying

In dying you won't find yourself going anywhere. You're just there. You are drawn mechanically to the atmosphere where you are able to vibrate. You won't see any odd things. There will be new things, but they will all be natural to you. You think of death as the entrance to an unknown world, but when you get there, you'll find it's not another world at all. The sphere of active life beyond the physical is all round you. One sphere of consciousness is superimposed on another. All are contained within each other, and are complementary, and stretched away into infinity.

Imagine that you are going to climb a mountain. Glasgow is at the foot. That is the physical world. As you climb, the air becomes rarefied. You reach a place a little cleaner. You go on into different conditions, each cleaner and more exhilarating than the last. You become eager to reach the top. Imagine that the mountain is forty thousand feet high, with a village at each one thousand feet, each more delightful than the last. They are all continuous, for there is no separation of the spheres.

If, by effort of will, you went down again, you would carry an impression of the places you had been in, and Glasgow would seem strange when you reached it. You would find that you could no longer dwell there. Your lungs would not be able to breathe the air, and the pavements would hurt your feet. The people would seem difficult and unexpected, vague and shadowy, as though they were in a fog. Your outer covering would have changed to suit the rarefied air.

The passing of the spirit from the body still spreads sorrow and gloom and unhappiness, both to those left behind and those who have made the change. People are not always prepared for death. They expect extraordinary changes, for they have ideas bred in them by the religions of the ages.

People who are aware of the reality of communication think that one has only to explain that life is continuous to change the whole world. That is not true. People may accept the facts of communication without getting a sense of continuity. They may also have ideas as to the future state of living, which are quite wrong. To become fully aware of life's continuity, it is more important to get alignment, or, at-oneness, with the Eternal Spirit, than to communicate through a medium.

Death is the opening of a door. It is a difficult opening for those unprepared, and we in Spirit are faced with the result of that lack of preparation. People on earth live in separate compartments, divided by religion, education, and so on. They don't understand those who live in different compartments and so are blinded to the true purpose of living. Many of them find that they have hardly lived at all, and are frightened by the force of life surging round them. Those who take hold of life with vigour after death, are those who have lived active, eager, forceful lives.

How eager we find the young soldiers and airmen! They quickly realise that death is not a matter of standing around, saying prayers and so on. It is a joy to see their relief, for they dreaded the heaven that had been portrayed to them. Their opportunities have trebled. There is nothing to tie them, so they go ahead as they wish. Like children learning to walk, they try to run, and fall and pick themselves up and go on again.

Some people think death is the end. When they find they are still alive, they have rather a problem. Some continue to hide from life and become utterly miserable in the process. They won't face the possibility of continuing life, so they pretend they are dead and live a miserable twilight existence.

Some are afraid. 'I was an atheist,' they say. 'I don't believe in life after death. I believe in the process of evolution. If I am still living, am I to be faced with God, priest, church that I've cleared my mind of? I'd rather die than be hidebound by religion.' He has to find a way out of his problem. Life stirs up the instinct of living in Spirit as on earth.

Rigorous believers in the doctrines of the church, heaven and hell, judgement day, Gabriel, Peter at the gate, and so on, tend to be arrogant in their beliefs. They demand to see Peter and the throne of God, and that they sit at His right hand. They have lived in their own compartment. To face the ordinariness of life is a great come down.

Elderly people expect heaven, and many of them sink into an apathy of disappointment, because the very naturalness of the place rules out heaven. They think something peculiar has happened to them. Some of them are angry, feeling they have been cheated. It takes time to rid oneself of these ideas of heaven and hell.

After death you can have a dull time if you are a dull person; you can be sad and lonely if you've been so important that you've thought no one is better than yourself, and very few as good. If you think your own family circle supreme, and shut out the warmth and brightness of other human love, you can be very lonely indeed. Life beyond death is determined by the conditions you impose on yourself.

To many people the stumbling block after death is that it is all so natural; the very naturalness makes them afraid. They realise a change has taken place, but don't realise what it is. When approached by friends, they think they are seeing ghosts. More experienced spirits who deliberately make themselves look and talk like these newcomers, meet and befriend them and help them to understand.

Life on earth is the first stage of the journey and you must now learn to live aright. You must all pass through the same experience of becoming spiritualised. Keep your mind and will flexible, and be willing to learn something new. Be able to learn from someone humbler than yourself, because your mind is still young.

After you come to our world, there is a period of awakening, when you cease to be dormant and become adjusted to your new environment. This period may be short, or it may last for years. When it arrives, you realise that coercion of the individual in every form has ceased. If master minds are at work, they are so wise that they are unseen.

You are, therefore, directed by your own aspirations to whatever interests you. If it is religion, you will, in the awakening period, realise that the old heaven just does not exist. What next? You will find many who pursue the same path as on earth, sure that they are still going towards the same goal. You will find concourses gathered for many different purposes, and you will discover a camaraderie greater than you ever before experienced.

After some time, you may reach a group and feel at home. You may find this group at once, or after a long search. You learn by meeting and pooling experiences. Imagine your friends in a fair landscape where there is sunshine, a soft breeze, flowers and companionship. They are sitting listening to talk concerning many aspects of life, perhaps a strange philosophy. Then, when there is the opportunity for questioning, they may find it difficult, feeling a little afraid of their own voices, or of sounding foolish, or of not expressing themselves clearly.

They meet again, drawn by the warmth of friendship, eager to learn under direction. Gradually they lose their sense of aloofness, and begin to get into the spirit of the thing. Those who have been trained, who have sat at the feet of the master, are in the position, not of teaching, or preaching, but of offering companionship. They sense the need of this one or that, giving the right word of encouragement, seeking out a particular difficulty, until there is perfect understanding in the whole gathering. Each is in tune with the other, and the gatherings continue on the basis of friendship and warmth.

When an enquirer is tutored, he becomes a disciple, and he in turn, seeks out those who are in need, perplexed perhaps by the strange new life they have entered, so different from any they had imagined. He uses gentle persuasion. He knows that some restorative power has cured his own ill. What is most effective is the friendliness of the gathering. Human understanding permeates the whole.

The most important thing in life is friendship and love. The soul can sink to depths, but only when it throws off the supporting and restraining power of love. The spirit is not immune from an influx of people battered on the rocks, mere wrecks on the stream of life. No power can change them one whit until someone can lead them by offering selfless love.

Those who love serve naturally. Love is the fundamental need of humanity. It is the only thing that matters in the next life. Spontaneity and goodwill and friendship are synonymous there.

P'shanta talks about activities in the Spirit World

Our world is one of activity. No one is happy doing nothing. It depends on the individual what activity he pursues. The newcomer is caught up in a whole range of exciting happenings, especially if he is a creative artist. Death, from whatever cause, brings to mentally alert persons such renewed vitality that a state of exhilaration appears, the newly dead being so much more alive than the living.

In the modern industrial state, there are many misfits who would be great assets if they could work in a different way: artists who are not able to work creatively; men with fine mental powers who must work repetitively; natural leaders who must work in a humble capacity. When such people come here and find there is no economic pressure forcing them to work, some of them run a little amok. Others are scared. They feel lost. Others, again, think it is a glorious opportunity, but soon they too feel lost because they have no training. They have to learn through experience.

When these people are acclimatised, they take up whatever interests them most. Some undergo severe discipline under guidance, to fit themselves for service. Others study arts or music, or find power in words. Some train to be leaders. That sounds impressive, but it is not, for it is a gradual growing, and the greatest is the humblest.

A newcomer to the Spirit World will gravitate first to his own family, many generations of it, more than he has any knowledge of. He will need to rest and feel secure, so he must be anchored somewhere. Each needs his own abiding place, and home will be ready for him.

After a time, he will want to explore the new world. Simply to live is an absorbing thing here, there is so much to learn. One can spend one's whole time in the sheer enjoyment of discovering new ways, meeting new people, reading new books. All history is written on the tablets of time. Everything worthwhile is recorded.

Eventually the time will come when the newcomer wants to do something in particular or enquire into something, and he finds his way to a group of people with whom he feels at home. If he is intellectual, he will seek intellectual people, if musical, people who enjoy music, and so on. In our world, people gravitate naturally to what is congenial to them. So, by enquiry, or seeming chance, the newcomer is led to where the best use of his talents can be made. Each pursues his own way. Not everyone enjoys it at first. To be happy one must find out the golden rule of service under direction.

P'shanta talks about the rules in the Spirit World

Our world is guided and directed by the people who inhabit it, just as yours is. We have no canon of laws, no punishment. Our laws are moral and spiritual, and we have a certain cure for the rebellious. It comes about naturally. Those who transgress find that they lose the warmth and friendliness they have enjoyed.

We live naturally and freely under a system of government quite different from yours. When people grow wise through finer living, they don't seek power, but rather set an example. Leaders are chosen by the people, really chosen. Someone wise and good and fine will naturally be elected to play his part in governance and guidance. Some people don't see advanced spirits such as these, because they live beyond their vibration. In the course of time, as one's perception grows, one becomes aware of those who are ahead of one.

P'shanta talks about development in the Spirit World

This earth is the place for partial or elementary growth. Even here a man can show his potentialities for greatness. For those who have used their potentialities for ill, after death, they will continue to use them in the same way, but they will become isolated. To begin with they will have a following of kindred spirits, disciples whom they will impress as they did on earth. But this will not satisfy them. They will wish to impress others whom they think more important, and they will find that these people are quite unimpressed, so they will begin to develop in a different direction.

There is no hierarchy. There is growth, either up or down. No one can stand still. It is through rising above his environment and inheritance that man has become what he is. Disappointment occurs frequently, especially disappointment with oneself. Hurt can come from people living on earth to whom one is bound by ties.

When a gifted person who has neglected his talent becomes stimulated, he will reach the edge of the circle that is right for him. One can become a pupil always. The creative urge is a driving force, the eternal seed of life. Suppose a great painter lost the desire to paint through dissolute and depraved living. After death he would enter his own particular hell for a bit, but eventually the creative fire would rise. The moment he raised his finger, help would be there.

P'shanta talks about awareness

Spirit people are psychically aware of what happens to their friends on earth, particularly those they are mentally in tune with. It is as if some vibrations were ringing a bell linking them with those they love, as though there were a telephonic impact. They use psychic awareness all the time, and see and hear, although they may be many miles from you.

They do not always find it possible to see you as you are. Many conditions, such as atmosphere and changes of environment, intervene. They must focus till they get the picture clear. If it goes out of focus, the vision is lost. Yet they are aware of most things concerning you. They are always linked with those they love, and can be instantly aware of their mental and emotional state.

5

TEACHINGS

P'shanta talks about God

Many people when they die are disappointed that they cannot see God. 'Who is God, and where is He?' they ask. The Spirit is everywhere, surrounding us. 'But,' they say, 'are we not created in the image of God, our Father?' They expect to ascend and see God visually.

I, P'shanta, cannot present God as a person. God has been the symbol of life continuing through many ages, a power beyond man's knowledge. In the acceptance of God, even an impersonal God, you are focussing on something beyond your ken, and convincing yourself that there is a force working for good.

I cannot say: 'I have found God,' and present Him to you. I can only tear veils down and say: 'Seek! Seek in the beauties of nature, in the mountains, trees and flowers, in the birds and the beasts, in the smile of a babe. There is wonder enough there, and life pulsating continuously.'

What gives inspiration to the poet? He must perceive God. He must come to the point of understanding and being uplifted, before his words will make mellow sound. A work of art is so because the artist's spirit has been uplifted and has brought back inspiration, a glimpse of what is beyond.

The spirit of life in you and in everything is God. Learn to see in all things a particle of that great Spirit which uplifts mankind towards God. In the attempt to find where God is, learn that the nearer to God, the nearer you are to your brother man. Among your fellows, find the real God that makes life worth living.

Man should think of himself as part of creation, part of the sun, moon and stars, one whole fellowship. He has to work towards his fulfilment, to go through an embryonic stage in his behaviour as well as physically. He must understand that all men are brothers.

Superstition and fear have caused many dark deeds. The predominant power of good is greater than of evil; but if the greater number of people desire evil, and desire it with a vigour, then evil will prevail. The powers of good and evil are inherent in man. He has developed them. It is his business in life to use his insight and divine ability to recognise the value of good and be guided by it.

You cannot live apart from evil. It is always with you, as good is. Do not shut yourself away from it so that you become a recluse. You cannot isolate yourself from evil any more than you can from germs. Recognise it for what it is, but let your armour be bright so that evil does not enter into you. In the same way, if you live a healthy life, infection will probably pass you by. If it does touch you, it won't kill you. It is part of everyday life to eschew evil, to eschew those things that are unhealthy and can leave in the mind only a smear. Your power to do so is greater than you think.

P'shanta talks about good and evil

Definition of 'being good'

Being at one with life and responding to that which is good: happiness. Happiness has the power to release forces in yourself.

There is no killing in the Spirit World, since there is no physical body, but there is always positive and negative. There is no life force without them. If we remain individuals, we must always have the power of good and evil, the choice between right and wrong. People on earth who lose the power to decide, are usually disordered mentally. The power to decide marks the individual.

If the power of evil holds away, it is because those who hold it are using it in a positive manner. If the power of good is used with the same strength and determination, it will be the ascendant power. Just being good is insufficient. It must be active goodness, strengthened by sympathy and knowledge. Be positively good. Active influences are the only ones which count.

Don't narrow the meaning of good and evil. They walk side by side with us all the time. Whenever things are at their best, something seems to happen to spoil them. You reach the zenith and then slide down. It is the evening of the scales. You can't remain static. While you are developing, you must obey the rhythm and keep reaching the zenith and coming down again. You can't always be very good, or stay on giddy heights for long. Life is meant to be up and down.

The positive and the negative run all through life. It is not only in man that there is good and evil. Plants give us poison as well as food. Some animals and birds are predators. In the Kingdom of God there are diversities, contradictions, affinities and enmities. Men themselves differ greatly. One can be a genius, or a great man leading nations; another may be corrupt, and lead others to corruption. How can God, if there be a God of peace and love, so distort His creatures?

When we look for God, we have to look for ourselves. Until we find God in ourselves, we do not know Him. You must find the quality and reality of God within yourself. God is not apart from life. Goodness is God. To attain spirituality, one must rise as close to God as one can. If people had a better idea of oneness with God, life would be simpler. You must realise the God within yourself. Think of God as the sun, so important to life, there can be none without it. We cannot set God apart. Everything pertaining to one's spiritual needs is in the godhead. We all know the essentials of goodness, for these have been taught to us in our childhood, but these teachings can be interpreted in many ways. Where can we find our anchor? Within ourselves, as God is.

P'shanta talks about losing one's way

You have strayed and don't know where you are going. You are on the borders of insanity, unity is broken. The bringing back, is the spirit (the noble side) finding the right road in aloneness (the way back to the fold of the self) so that you are physically knit in yourself; back from the mists and hells of loneliness, mistrust and misapprehension. You stand renewed. Mind, body and spirit are one. It is only when one is in harmony that one is really sane. Sanity means perfect balance, perfect health, in body, mind and spirit.

P'shanta talks about forgiveness

If you are truthful, you will realise that you harbour many things against people who have harmed you. This harbouring is the real ill they have caused. Before you pray, make sure you forgive. Pray for the will to deliver yourself to goodness from evil. 'I do not, will not see evil. Deliver me, myself, from the evil that is within me.' That is: 'I am determined to deliver myself from evil.'

P'shanta talks about tolerance

Is tolerance just a lack of disagreement, the acceptance of something without acrimony? To me, tolerance is understanding the other person's point of view. I am afraid that you substitute indifference, the mere acceptance without complaint, for tolerance. Some things I strongly object to, but I have learned to object without injuring myself. I never allowed myself to become the victim of someone else's intolerance.

Everyone has the right to think for himself, and to air his opinion, but tolerance seems to you to hinge on not enforcing your views on others. To me, the attributes of tolerance are not confined to that. The tolerance which comes of more perfect understanding is the will to remain unshaken, however difficult anyone may be and however strongly they may try to break your defence. If you can be swayed against your better judgement, then you are weak somewhere.

You accept many things because they are enforced upon you by circumstances. Your conscience is only developed by your mental and physical environment and so your viewpoint is tinged. You do not call things by their true names. If you are honest thinkers, you will realise that you are often guided by expediency.

Intolerance in the real sense is the inability to change. Though a person may be dogmatic on some occasions, he is not necessarily an intolerant person. A really intolerant person is intolerant in all things. His mind is clouded by prejudice. There is no shaft of light cleansing and purging his mind. He is usually a doleful person thinking only of himself.

But the tolerant person has a mind open to the sun and wind. He accepts the impositions placed upon him with understanding and never loses his sense of humour. He is biddable, teachable, lovable. He can see his house knocked down and set about building it up again.

Poise and serenity are necessary for your peace of mind and happiness. These do not come from a tolerant acceptance of evil, but from a surety of your own behaviour in life. Poise is the tolerance which life has taught you, a tolerance towards all striving creatures.

P'shanta talks about facing challenge

Remember that people may smite you from various causes. They may resent that you are being good to them, not because they don't want you to be good to them, but because it may show them in rather a bad light. They may be embarrassed, or their feelings may be in a hypersensitive state, so they metaphorically smite your cheek.

Giving you a council of perfection, I would say that goodness and nobility has its own defence, and in the dignity of it, one wouldn't want to smite back. One would have the self-discipline to remain calm. All these injunctions to good behaviour come near to the counsel of perfection, the strict discipline of the self towards the perfect control of mind over body and spirit.

'Love your enemies, do good to them that hate you.' That may seem impossible, but don't let that worry you. If your enemy were in distress, would you help him? The motivating power of love is there if you would help him without feeling aggrieved or self-righteous.

P'shanta talks about 'the meek'

You interpret meekness as being demure and quiet and afraid to talk back. It doesn't mean that at all. A meek person means someone who is not proud, that is, not proud of being good or righteous, one who can appreciate the impulses and idiosyncrasies of other people, who has the same understanding heart, and can see through the pretensions people are constantly displaying, but who does not seek to discountenance them, or to cause unhappiness.

P'shanta talks about being 'master of yourself'

If you are master of yourself, you are master of your own kingdom. You accept the laws of life and are secure in the knowledge that you are in control of yourself. The kingdom of the spirit is inviolate if you know how to guard it. We have to inherit our own little earth.

The earth is wide and we know there is much going on in it that we don't like. There are many places that we should like to see, but cannot, for one reason or another. We can read of them and their history, and we know that there are all sorts of men.

Yet our own little part in life is our kingdom, which we must learn to inherit. You might say of one who is blind, or deaf, or paralysed: 'What has he got on the earth to inherit?' It would surprise you if you knew some of these people and the wonderful kingdom they've inherited because of their own efforts. They not only see without the physical eye, hear without ears, and move without limbs. They do all these things and many more because they've inherited the kingdom of God that is within them.

You have each a very precious kingdom. Above all, you have the gift of intelligence. Use it, and not for one thing only. Remember that you enlarge your kingdom by using your intelligence, and portraying for yourself that which you need most. Many of the things that were taught you in childhood stand you in good stead because you've absorbed them as a plant does sunshine and light, air and water.

You must not make heavy weather of disciplining yourself. Some people join orders and may go through very doubtful disciplining. You are wise enough to know that you are far from perfect and that nobody expects you to be perfect.

Distinguish between morbid self-immolation and unselfish service to others. True unselfishness gives a width of view. To be really good and selfless, one must be so unconsciously.

To feel strong, you must ask for strength and for spiritual food and water, and the things that keep you spiritually whole. You are an immortal soul and you have to progress through many years in this life, and then after death, for many, many more in the spirit life, before you reach perfection. You are endowed with all the potentialities needed to make you feel that perfection will one day be within your grasp.

Retain your freedom of thought, of love, of generosity. Life here is a preparatory school. If you don't learn its lessons, you will have difficulty later in accepting the finer state you will enter into. Reaching perfection takes a long time, and you should enjoy your progress towards it. Nothing worthwhile is easy.

Gather to yourself peace. Be gentle even if people are cross with you. It's easy to do a big good thing. It's harder to do a lot of little things that no one will notice. A true generous spirit is never conscious of doing something good. He does it because love is in his heart.

P'shanta talks about prayer

Long ago, back through ages of time, man devised idols built in the image of himself, that he might conduct ceremonies of praise and prayer, of initiation and wonder, and of miracles. Always it has been necessary for man to have something other than his own powers to bolster himself against the world.

Floods or catastrophes have been the work of devils or gods, according to the occasion, or the mood of the people. Man must have a focal point to which he can address his prayers and his wishes for good and ill, for the nurture of his flocks and the increase of his cattle, and for his defence against enemies and storms and other calamities.

When the way of life is fair, man remembers to pray, but he does not understand the completeness of prayer, or his ability to use it. When the sky is dark, anguish catches him, and he cries aloud, fearing that God has forsaken him. He does not, nowadays, seek the best and dearest thing he has to lay on the altar as an offering, but he stands before God and prays aloud.

To every soul come many moments, the height and depths of experience, joy and anguish, which can loosen the spirit so that it finds wings and flies. That is prayer; it releases you. Its potency depends on the strength of the individual desire. A soul stirred to the depths has stood at the gateway and been given power to ascend or descend. The very act of prayer is an ascendancy of the self. Accustom yourself to pray, to know that the storehouse, where all is true spirit and goodness, is always accessible.

When you pray, don't be a suppliant or see yourself as a creature buffeted by winds. Go and find what you need. Don't ask for mercy or forgiveness unless you are sure you are repentant and willing to atone. If you have done something you are ashamed of, do not pray: 'Forgive me,' but rather: 'May I be permitted to undo the harm I have wrought.'

If you pray for strength, be ready to go forward. If you pray for peace, do something to build a temple for peace to dwell in. Prayer must always be away from the self; not: 'Make me good,' but rather: 'Let me make me good; let me make me strong so that I may be fitted to draw from life my need.'

Prayer is a natural instinctive thing. It has nothing to do with your picture of God, or with what God is. When one is in difficulties, when one is afraid, when one is in despair, one prays. All people, of whatever nationality, or colour, have this instinctive thing, prayer. That means that all men acknowledge something outwith themselves, supreme in power and wisdom. In effect, they say: 'I am the imperfect thing. There is something beyond me to which I reach out.'

Man has been taught to pray to God, a God outside himself, a God that is perfect in all things. To some, he is fierce, to some, a mixture of fierceness and loving kindness, to some, a God of love. But the supremacy, the oneness of God is accepted and prayers are offered to Him.

In reality, one's prayer is an outpouring of the self which is seeking succour in the finer state of life. It is the desire that something will come to the self from without, to give it the strength and ability to reach the help it seeks, not only for the self, but for others.

The prayer is sometimes directed to God in the sense of trying to placate, or to ask for the improvement of the self. It may even be a display of self-righteousness. You must learn to pray aright. Rid yourself of the idea of 'saying a prayer', but pray with the whole force of your being. Don't think of praying to a God who will accept or reject, but think of yourself as part of the godhead, able to resurge yourself continuously with its power. Outside yourself is the whole kingdom of good for you to use if you know how, and your prayer is an attempt to touch part of your future kingdom. Find yourself, but lose yourself too in the immensity of time.

Prayer, real prayer, is very fine and very necessary. Without it, one cannot hope to find that which is outwith oneself, outwith one's immediate knowledge, but which is in truth part of oneself. Prayer can express the longing, the desire, the willingness to absorb that which is good. Even if your prayer is only a cry for help out of bewilderment, or great sorrow and distress, it is still pouring forth into that unknown whence help may come.

One, overcome with grief, prays and gets a release of emotion, something undefined, translated into words, and help comes because he is able to see more clearly. He has cleft a way out. He has reached something real, and in the outpouring of grief, has found an immediate answer to prayer.

If you express your longings in prayer, you help yourself to become what you desire. As you worship what is far from you, you become mute in admiration. Whether prayer is silent, or spoken in public, it is on every occasion an offering to fulfil oneself to perfection. It is very valuable because it sets off a chain reaction and forms links with others both on earth and in Spirit. It is a living thing, a part of your soul. It has an outward and inward wave. You project it and bring in what you desire.

Prayer is less the seeking of the miraculous than an attempt to find the source of one's own being, and to create something out of the prayer: the release of a spring, a soaring of the spirit, perhaps an unconscious impact, which, coming into the conscious mind, can help you to think things out. It is petition to a force beyond yourself, which is yet part of you. It loosens that which is 'you' and allows you to acquire for yourself that which you seek. In its highest form, you pray: 'May I become perfected so that I may perceive the glory of God; may I be stilled that peace embrace me; may I experience joy, so that purest joy shall enthral me, that in all things I may experience the fullness of life.'

Prayer is an uprising of the self, a purging of the spirit. It is often spontaneous and undirected, a cry from the heart. If it is dynamic, it is potent and can bring either good or evil in its train. It is difficult for you to get away from the idea that prayer can only be good, but that is not so. Every desire, good or evil, is a prayer. People pray for all sorts of things, but every good, unselfish thought towards another is an imperishable jewel. Good can spread through thought as well as through action, and nothing that is good is ever lost.

You pray for another, but nearly always the prayer concerns yourself as closely. That is natural in the human ego. The strongest prayers are those by people in immediate need. It takes great love and selflessness to pray as earnestly for another.

You can never be told that something will come right because you pray, nor is it possible to have confirmation of the effectiveness of prayer. Thought is like thistle down. It goes from you, but you can't trace where every segment has gone. The seeds scatter, providing for the resurrection of something somewhere.

Suppose you seek help for a friend who is ill. Consider the recipient. It depends upon him whether your prayer will help or not, for there is a receiving as well as a sending out. By your own vitality, send a thought to your sick friend: 'You are capable of restoring yourself. Be well. Unite yourself to the origin of life.'

His thoughts and yours may then unite, and the energising power of prayer will be evident as restoration takes place. Your prayer must be selfless. Even so, there may be barriers to it, for prayers are not miraculously fulfilled. It takes the drawing together of several forces to make strong the power that can bring about what you have prayed for.

Don't pray for the impossible. There was an idea abroad in 1944 (Second World War) that prayer would bring peace. That is not a reasoned prayer. Consider first what causes war, and change these conditions. The true prayer for peace is a prayer for the ability to do something to promote peace. Any other prayer is futile expenditure of emotion, and emotion alone is no great asset, although, reasoned disciplined emotion is good and creative.

When you pray for those unknown to you, like prisoners of war, you must learn to create such a bond of sympathy and love that your prayer will reach its objective. Those capable of hatred cannot create such a bond. You must start by looking within yourself and getting your own reaction into true perspective, so that you know these for what they are, and can distinguish reality from pretence. Learn to feel compassion and sympathy, pity and love, for those you may feel you should hate as enemies. If you wish the regeneration of others, you must be able to feel love for all mankind, and to abnegate yourself in the interest of another.

The need for prayer will not die with your physical body. You will still pray, you will still desire, you will still find many difficulties that will be best answered through your prayers. Pray earnestly every day. You must get into the right attitude, into the quiet serenity of it, very restful, very precious. Get the feeling of being in touch with good, with God if you will. Reach the sanctity of knowing that the outpouring of your heart is going beyond yourself, outside your narrow circle of physical conditions. It is the forming of a chain, or more picturesquely, a rainbow, a promise that is lighting things up for you, and through the feeling of calmness and lightness your prayer is answered almost before you are aware of it.

One should pray often. In the midst of toil and worry and disturbance just stand still a minute and pray. It will help you enormously. I most strongly emphasise the importance of prayer from the soul, prayer for oneself and for others.

I like to think of prayer being an integral part of all of you, the self, trying to express the innermost part of one's being, at times stuttering brokenly, but always praying earnestly. Commune with yourself. Pray without ceasing. Learn to acquire a poise which will light a flame within an inner ascendancy. True prayer is active and helps you to grow in spirit.

P'shanta talks about mental and physical health

You must try to think of the things that will give you a better perspective upon life. I find, talking with people, that the stress of life, today, is so accelerated, the mental pressure is so great, there are so many 'buts' and 'ifs' and conditions that don't seem to form into a regular pattern, that they become distressed. More people than ever seem to be tired, and finding things difficult: and even the everyday ordinary things that happen in all people's lives seem to be more difficult to cope with than before.

The mental field that encircles your life (I might say, quite truly encircles the earth), is something which touches you: though you aren't always aware of it, unless you are more receptive. When you express your own feelings about the stresses of life, you are expressing an indication of the general trend of things that are happening today. The stress will not break suddenly, so it is important that you learn how to take care of your spirit, your soul: for they become jaded too. You live in a complicated condition. There are many things little understood by the ordinary person.

They see things that are directly in line with their vision. Some think very little ahead. Some seek solace by rushing more, keeping busy so they can't think.

First things first: look at your health. Your physical body is the important vehicle of expression for you now, and mentally and physically, you want to be in tune. In nature there is, as you know, constant renewing of the essences and the conditions for life. No matter what form of life exists (human, beast, bird, or flower), there must be continuous renewing of the vehicle through which the spirit must function. However, the spiritual side of man is so often neglected. If, however, you are in tune with yourself, you'll find you'll be better able to come into tune with others. If the body is sick, the mind follows suit. You can't think clearly and you can't decide clearly. It is therefore very important to try and determine the right way of living.

When life was less hurried than it is today, man produced more in the way of art and literature; also, music, painting and great architecture. Today, man shuts his eyes to the real impulses that guide his creative forces. Most of the real pleasures of life come straight from simple things, but we adjust our bodies to the conditions of modern life. I am sure that most people are more fatigued and restless than they can ever remember being. They put this down to age: but that is just an excuse. The condition of your mind and body affects others, and their conditions affect you.

As you grow out of the middle years, there will be things that slow you down, but physically, not with your mind. If you find that you are not remembering things, then that is a sign that you have lost tune with a very important part of yourself. You must rest your mind. You can rest your mind and restore its powers by doing absolutely nothing: but that in itself can take an effort.

We are all occupied with something during the day: children, work, other people. You can however start with ten minutes, then fifteen, even half an hour. Time to close your eyes and rest yourself, thinking quietly of the loveliest things you can remember. Perhaps an excursion you made with somebody like yourself with the hills and the rivers and the wooded places: and perhaps the song of a bird. You might even fall asleep, and that is the very best medicine for a tired mind and body.

And Spirit: does it need to rest? Yes!

I wonder how successful I would be in my work if I never got rid of the conditions I pick up whilst contacting you people. I would be of no use to you if I didn't pick them up: and I pick them up because of the porous way we operate. I cannot stand aloof from you any more than you can stand aloof from me. I want you to realise that the most important thing is to repair yourself, but not just in a physical way. What your eyes and ears take in, is absorbed by your soul, somewhere, and it is the spiritual mind that cleanses this.

P'shanta talks about symbolism and fire and water

Many things which are regarded as mere symbolism have a foundation in reality. We have lost much ancient lore. We dwell in comparative safety from the elements; we no longer build our own houses for shelter; we don't convert the conditions of nature to our own requirements; we've forgotten the importance of fire. We only know it is necessary for our physical well-being, to cook food, to give us warmth. So, too, with water. We don't know what it means to be without it. Water and fire are indispensable to man, and a great deal of ancient lore has been built up round them. Ritualists say that incorporated in it there is truth. You can't separate fire and water from man; therefore, they are part of the ritual of life.

Too many people are afraid of tracing things back to their origin. It is right to be guarded against superstition, but it is good to sift, from superstition, ancient truths and mould them to rules of conduct. Fire can cleanse, purge and destroy. It can allow things to pass through it and become changed and separated. In modern life, that is well known. Things are now built up from the separations caused by fire.

People of ancient times worshipped both fire and water in their own way. They were afraid of fire. They had not learned to master it. So, too, with water. Houses are no longer engulfed in flooded rivers. Man must copy nature (beavers) because the constructive quality of nature shows man how to use his powers. He becomes an engineer because nature is a great engineer; a mathematician because nature is a great mathematician.

Nature and you are one and indivisible. Your physical being originates from nature. There are laws which control crystallisation, fertility, colour: all the phenomena hidden in earth. Man has seen and learned from nature all that is necessary for his welfare. In spite of religionists, man cannot continue to live unless he is part of the kingdom of nature. His heavens and hells must be within the kingdom of his own living. Most of the conditions borrowed from nature by man have fundamental laws at their base. Better to enquire patiently into ancient beliefs, than to destroy them out of hand.

Water is necessary to our being. Man in ancient times naturally worshipped it, and found it in gods. Who, watching a cascade, could not but feel in the presence of a mighty force? If you do not blend with it, you become afraid. No one should fear water because it is merged in all people. It is necessary to drink water. Think of water from the aesthetic and occult senses. It is you. You can see in water: cleansing; purification; strength; wisdom; and vitality. Even domestic water can become different if you perceive it with an eye which unites it to your kingdom: and you to its kingdom.

Water has uses in a hidden esoteric sense. Make a ritual and significance of your cleansing. Make it part of your daily routine, not only because it is good for your health, it has greater importance than that. A ritual cleansing: a preparation of the psychic self which is being cleansed by the power of the universe. The daily bath is a very important ritual. So is a glass of water when you need a cool draught. It is important to you. Your soul needs it, and you can use it daily for this purpose. If in a summer walk in the country you came to a stream, it will attract you. Let the attraction be mutual. Bathe your feet. Remember, you are going to water, and it is coming to you. It is a union, a service. Water is a friend, a protector, a stimulator, part of nature, the cosmos, the universe.

P'shanta talks about the art of discussion

How many of you have learned the art of discussion: the give and take of good argument? How many of you can find the right centre of the matter discussed? Do you know what people do in Spirit? They do a lot of talking and discussing.

Imagine yourselves a group gathered together for this purpose. You have passed a few remarks. Someone brings up a point, and a most enlightened discussion takes place, and you go away refreshed. Could you do that?

Do you find it easier to swim with the tide of thought today? Do you accept readily the things you hear? What do you think is the predominant philosophy today? A sure philosophy is so important that it governs all that we do. It can change as one grows in experience. You must experiment until you find the philosophy which suits you.

Some people have an evil philosophy. In politics, for example, your lives are determined by the philosophies prevailing in the political arena. There is no urge, at the moment, to delve into the rights and wrongs of things. Some people, by propaganda, call attention to the wrongs. But if the prevailing philosophy is such that they are going against it, their efforts will not be seen. Things will be brought forward to disprove what they say. People believe the newspapers. Your own philosophy should promote good thoughts, for the power of thought is very influential. Your thought is you. The more you think about yourself in the right way, the better you will be. Do not do things for righteousness' sake, but because the heart dictates it.

P'shanta talks about the physical world in 1938

The people of the earth are faced with potential war. They are crying towards God that the conditions of earth may alter and that there may be sent into their midst a saviour, or saviours, who will deliver them. It is always the same. From the midst of the people, must there rise someone who will command the people and lead them: and as the good can arise, so can those arise who understand not the power that they have at their command, and who do not save, but who lead for evil.

Selfishness is the bane of mankind. Man becomes occupied with himself to the exclusion of others. It is a very difficult thing to understand exactly how to think of yourself, and yet understand that you must not be concerned with your physical self all the time. The combination of the physical and the spiritual is so mixed that you have to understand the differences between the two if you want to live well and truly. So many of you live very beautiful lives, very simply. You do your best every day.

When you see the things that people do are not to your liking, send a little prayer. Do not in your mind think ill of them, because that ill is coming from yourself. Think good, think wisely: and think well. May the Great Father of us all hearken to our prayer, as we pray from the depths of our being, that our souls may be gilded with the sun of Thy Glory. May thou shine upon us, that we may join in the great throng that sings praises unto Thee. Surround us with the great white light of Thy Majesty, and give us wings that we might soar into places of the true soul, and there find contentment and rest. Help us to give that we may be given unto. Help us to become humble that we may become great, and help us to serve that others may serve us.

May thy love surround us all and those to whom our hearts are akin, that we, shining in this darkened world, may cause a light that will draw into it all those who desire to live truly; may woe and sadness soon pass from the world, and may man be alive to the strength within: and may he realise that unless he is good and kind, his living is of no avail.

P'shanta talks about the effects of war on spiritual and physical evolution

The ability to send helpful thoughts is essential. To be effective, we must have confidence in our powers, have a picture of the invalid and environment in our minds, be willing to give something of ourselves, and be able to fasten on to the desire we wish to send.

With regard to war, thoughts of peace are not enough. Unfortunately, the stronger in war will win, so that the laying down of arms is ineffective. We must be ready to sacrifice and to endure, as others have done before, remembering that it is in our power to prevent the occurrence of war. Many factors come into play, and there are fundamentals to change.

Evolution is a slow process. Things don't happen suddenly. Many evils are due to maladministration in industry. There is also the tragedy of the old who are not provided for. Overcrowding in cities; lack of sympathy and an absence of community makes them question the purpose of life. So, what is it that represents satisfaction with life? Enough money? Think of the earth: all you need for physical sustenance is there. None should be denied it. Primitive man received all he wanted: sun and food.

As man develops, he becomes more sensitive to joy and pain. When spiritually attuned, he can attain greater heights. Life cannot be divided into compartments. We should understand the whole. You must be students and delve into the history of mankind. Don't leave things to others to manage for you: you must see the whole of life.

Every age shows the tendency of life to evolve. Men don't understand how they retard by their slothfulness. New ideas are spurned. Every true reformer should be aided by those who think. You must not decry them, unless you have examined what they say. Don't be an echo of another: be yourself.

Necessity to live is the greatest factor to war. If you are attuned to your spirit, knowledge makes you understand how to truly live. But the initiative has been taken from you. Do you now think for yourself, or, is your thinking done for you? Are you a free people? Man is building the chariot that is drawing him to his doom. You must think out the remedy yourself.

Sensuality isn't life, nor are physical pleasures enduring. What spurs man on is his spirit. What advantage is science if man is turned into a baser metal? Life must take on simpler contours. Don't assess life by money, or by possessions: unless it is the work of a craftsman. Put into your work something of yourself. If you are wearied at night, it is because you have missed some of the spiritual things. Go and find what your spirit needs. Don't ask for mercy or forgiveness. Don't see yourself as weak. Do something to help and get a knowledge of brotherhood.

Within the human soul are wonderful powers. They are apparent within a person: they are part of him. They belong to God and are divine. But unless these powers are developed and utilised, they remain hidden and create dissatisfaction within the soul. Such powers could relate to mediumistic skills, or art, singing, architectural design and more. These are all powers that belong to the soul. They are powers that can make others happy. To seek to pursue only the path of mediumistic development is wrong: it should be noted that there are others out there, who through their own earnest efforts, reach prominence in their own art, showing that they have also become suitable instruments to help and benefit mankind.

Relying on others instead of oneself creates discontent. In the Spirit World, you will find that you increasingly rely on yourself. You will find that it is your own initiative you are dependent on. Most certainly, you will find helpful comradeship and friendship: and this will be something more wonderfully precious than you have ever imagined. In the Spirit World there are many people, who having developed their own particular power, when merged together, become a perfect pattern, and each enjoys the power of the other. There is no debating on whether one person is as good as the other, or whether one can do a certain thing better than the other. Can't you imagine all the component parts fitting into the scheme, perfectly wonderful with colours that give you the feeling of ecstasy? Where sound vibration is only beautiful, and where your whole soul is basking in the light and becomes animated and uplifted and drawn towards that perfect thing: the Creator of the Whole.

You must start at the beginning. You must use your powers and make yourself actively engaged upon the pursuit of peace, because in pursuing peace, you will gather round all the conditions that belong to the peaceful state. When you pursue a course of studies, and you are earnest about reaching your goal, you apply yourself very diligently to the task. If you want to progress spiritually, allowing your soul to become a strong partner, you must make every effort to understand the necessary conditions. You have to make yourself aware of what the real things in life are, and not be disturbed by annoyances.

Try to gain peace within yourself, for until each individual understands peace, all the preaching of peace for mankind will be of little avail. The things of life that rush at you, do not engender peace. They have the opposite effect of generating disturbances that do a great deal to you. They even have the power to destroy your physical body: your mind, upset by these things, can have a devastating effect on your physical frame, but mind can also reverse that process, so let your soul develop.

P'shanta talks about health and healing

The ordinary individual, who does not understand the makeup of his physical body is dependent entirely upon how he feels, and he trusts somebody who has superior knowledge to prescribe for him, and to tell him the ruling that is best for good health. The health of the body is dependent very much on the health of the mind: although the mind may be impaired, and the ordinary functions of the body go on very successfully and correctly fulfilling their duties.

You have the biologist, who studies and endeavours to understand the makeup of the physical body. He tries to understand the different things that attack it and that would seek to destroy it. You have the physiologist who understands all about the organs of the body and their reactions upon one thing and another; and you have the psychologist who, included in the profession of the medical man, is a very definite asset to the fuller understanding of the whole. To attempt to go over the whole field of health, of course, would be too great a task in a little space of time, but as it looms so importantly in front of you, it is very necessary to understand a little of what your body can perform, and your duty to help your body.

Now, there are many claims made that mind being the superior force, it should right every ill within the body. Perhaps that is, in the main, correct, but when talking to people who do not understand the importance of the mind, it is an extraordinarily strong statement to make. In fact, it very often distresses the person who is suffering from some ill, because of his lack of knowledge of his mystic self. And so, we find that many people suffer ill health for many years without discovering a cure. It is left to the medical man with his specialised knowledge to discover for you the cause of your physical ill, but medical men will be the first to admit that there is so much in the human body, so many reactions, so many glandular activities, so many contradictions of what should normally be, that they, themselves, are in many instances lost because of their inability to understand the actual influences of the various organs in the body.

Now, we have got to remember the combination of all these things, so that we can arrive at some idea of what each should aim at in trying to induce the body to work more perfectly. Not many people understand, or have been taught, that heredity plays an important part in their health. That is generally accepted, but it requires a great deal of qualification.

One of the most important things in the body, or, shall we say, the most vital thing in the body, is the blood stream. Probably you would expect me to say that the heart is the most important, but you will find that the blood stream is more important. It is through the blood stream that inherited predisposition arises; and the heart, being the organ that acts under the will of the nervous system and the subconscious mind of the individual, will perform its duty from infancy to old age in a perfect manner if the blood stream remains all that time, pure.

That which makes up the blood stream has to go through many changes before it reaches the vital organ, the heart, and if the other organs in the body do not do their duty correctly, then the heart is left to deal with all the impurities that the other organs in the body should deal with, and these enemies collect and destroy. They interfere with action, they destroy the important muscles and they do a great deal of harm, until the individual is told that his heart is diseased. What has happened is this: the heart has been unable to withstand the strain and the impositions placed upon it, and so it fails to do its work. Sometimes an individual, from the very beginning, will suffer impairment of certain organs through prenatal causes. These cannot be explained in a small attempt to outline the ordinary rulings of health. These organs remain impaired usually through life.

As there is in all life the rule of compensation, so does the rule of compensation go on inside your own physical body. You must remember, of course, there are many instances where, without the skill of the surgeon and his timely interference, the life flow of the individual (the blood stream) would not be able to flow through the body at all, and so physical life would cease.

Those who study the conditions requisite for perfect health have, in the last century, done an enormous amount of good work. They have taught the people the necessity for hygiene. They have taught them that it is important to consider the conditions in which a healthy body should be nurtured. They have studied, very often at the risk of the impairment of their own health, that they might give to a world, which was gradually becoming the inheritors of many new and strange diseases, a new outlook on life.

They have, through their research, destroyed almost altogether the possibility of infection through lack of hygiene. Many of those things come within our knowledge, and yet people continue to suffer through mismanagement of their own organs. There is a very important rule of health, and it is this: if everything is working in perfect harmony together, then you are hardly aware of your body. It is perfectly able to look after itself and perform through that monitor which is the subconscious mind of the individual.

Now we have come to a very important thing: the nervous system. It is through the nervous system that you are aware, through pain, or discomfort, that there is need to attend to something within the organism. The individual, after receiving the signals, attempts to repair the damage. If he ignores these warnings, life will be impaired and endangered. Emotions also affect our bodies. They can assist or hinder: and anger will hinder any healing process.

One of the most valuable things that you possess is the ability to be perfectly tired. The body is dependent upon renewing and exhausting different things within it, and it is the working of the physical body that allows things to ebb and flow. It allows the free expansion of the lungs, so that the body may be kept in physical wellbeing. But there is a certain amount that the nervous system can stand, and beyond that, it will rebel.

People forget that they can get too tired. When they get overstrained, they lose that feeling of wellbeing. Sleep then instead of being the natural function it is (health giving and life preserving) does not act in that way, and the person who is over tired does not wake from sleep feeling restored.

I have studied the needs of the physical body for a long time. Health ought to be easy to attain, provided you are willing to attend to your body's demands in a sensible manner. Learn to eat wisely. When you eat wrongly, your body suffers: so, you should stop this to restore the balance. If you are tired, and cannot get restoration through sleep, then your body is being starved of what it needs. Listen to your body.

6

MEDIUMSHIP
AND PSYCHIC CONNECTIONS

P'shanta talks about psychic perception

Incidents in our lives leave scars on the psychic self, particularly traumatic events. Such things can be seen by others through psychic perception. Something indelible has been created in the psychic self. If you were to consult me regarding your health, I must see your physical body internally. In the same way I can see you psychically, and see the scars on your psychic self. Your emotional life, your will, your struggles, your weaknesses and so on are there for people like me to see clearly.

Most people use their psychic perception unconsciously, and so it is called by many queer names: inspiration, for example. When you meet a new acquaintance and feel a sudden bond of sympathy, or experience revulsion towards him, you are using your psychic perception.

Any emotional crisis stands out like a deep scar. Shocks all leave their mark. People talk of the 'recording angel'. You are each your own recording angel. When you live entirely in that field of active life which draws from the psychic, these scars are gradually ironed out, as if you were able to cast skins, and eventually you become really beautiful.

Emotions, even good ones, should always be well controlled. To be too angry, or even too sympathetic, is unwise. So many people sympathise in the wrong way, and make the one they sympathise with feel worse rather than better. Be temperate in all things and extreme in none. Value your own judgement and by true knowledge of yourself learn to value the potentialities of another.

P'shanta talks about developing our psychic self

The soul has been defined as 'the other man': the one with the power to create. Creating is the greatest action of man. It is the response to that great spiritual urge in all of us. We create both spiritual and physical things.

Preordained destiny is not true. Man plans and creates his own destiny. He is the arbitrator of his fate. We are now laying the foundations of a new generation. Knowledge of the psychic self will enable one to advance enormously. Man has the power to benefit from the well of accumulated knowledge: also, to travel into another source of wisdom.

Everyone possesses psychic power. No one is purely physical. Many are frustrated in childhood from developing their psychic power, when dreams or incredulous fantasies have been discouraged. Only those who can project this psychic power into something creative, are accommodating this power with the physical body. We should think in an orderly way and find the best medium for the release of our psychic power: not necessarily in art, literature or painting. Just something ordinary related to day-to-day duties.

The secret of youthful living is joy. Joy in accomplishment, and joy in getting other people to create. The body is wonderful. It is able to renew itself by cell growth and more. It has the power to be well. Infuse joy into mundane things. Create, create and create again. In the Spirit World everything must be created by yourself. You cannot possess other people's creations. Only through created effort can you own things.

Be aware of what is going on around you. Draw benefits and comforts from nature round you. Be able to discern the true forces of nature within you: and see your relation to your brother. Acquire knowledge. Cease to think of the body for sensual enjoyment alone. A redirection of thought power is required for improvement. Every action of life should be a living act.

Teach the young the rudiments of psychology rather than religion. Most mental ills are due to ignorance of self. Think about yourself and your imperfections. Allow your parts to blend: physical and spiritual. Your first duty is to yourself.

P'shanta talks about religion

There is much to be said about religion: both the good and the evil of it. Man is a contrary being. He can be good when he learns the power to choose wisely. But he is variable. Man has always believed in powers outside himself, partly because he didn't understand the forces of nature, afraid only when they were beyond his control.

These forces became his gods, and fearing that they might destroy him, he prayed to them. If his prayers were unanswered, he thought the gods were angry with him, and this concept became the start of religion. From this, it may be supposed that religion was founded on ignorance and superstition. But there is an alternative consideration: man had instinctive knowledge of the forces around him that he could draw on, and drawing on them was his right.

Churches of today house the gods of man's own creation, but why is there a distinction of the same fundamental needs? Why sects? Why competition? Man has become shackled by religion and is no longer free to roam. No single person can claim one bit of superiority over another, by ritual, or otherwise. Only individual need can dictate one's way to find the outlet for his spiritual emotion to make and find his own God. The wise, who have passed to the Spirit World, will tell you that they create according to their needs: the desire for life to express itself more and more all the time. That is the only religion.

The greatest force is life force. Kindness and nobility are worthier than a temple. Who is better? The free man, or, the man, afraid, who follows the priests? Man should not pray to a god fashioned by another. He should free himself from the shackles of a thousand years. As man improves his mind, he usually frees himself. Live and create, and let your brother express himself in his own way.

P'shanta talks about dependence on spirit friends

Believing that our spirit friends can tell us everything that is going to happen, is wrong. It is a harmful belief. It weakens one's self-reliance and makes the individual dependent on advice from those in Spirit on matters which require one's own judgement. Such dependence becomes a habit, where the individual will do nothing without first consulting spirit friends.

Such people have really no idea what communication means. We forge a chain to reunite the worlds so that man shall realise that he is a spirit, and finding strength and new impetus from that realisation, shall gain an ascendancy over himself. Mediumship is not a vehicle for fortune-telling. Another aspect of dependence on spirits is the assumption that they can perform miraculous cures. This is also wrong. Spirit people cannot do the impossible.

P'shanta talks about mediumship

When there is mediumship, especially trance, there must be a guide and controls. There is much confusion in the use of these words. In any developed mediumship, there is one guide. He is the person who looks after the medium and directs the work done. He may also work as a control.

It is the duty of a guide, solemnly undertaken after dedicated preparation, to link through a medium with people who will learn to trust and love him. Thereby, he renders true service, drawing on his wealth of experience and wisdom to assuage grief, and to teach, restore and encourage all who will listen to him. At the same time, he inevitably sacrifices the enjoyment of his own true environment.

The guide must be wise and very patient. He must have knowledge of all the conditions of the medium, such as the brain, the nerve centres and the blood stream. He must be aware of the reactions to trance and be master of the situation at all times.

In physical mediumship, the guide will direct the work and keep harmful things out. He will be close to the medium, but not often in control. On occasion he may interrupt the proceedings, and even end them if, for example, the medium is overtired, or the power is being too much used.

He has the welfare of the medium always at heart. Anything that occurs during the functioning of mediumship is his concern and he is consulted on all things pertaining to it. Noise, light and interruptions are all detrimental to mediumship. If the guide is firmly established, he can minimise the danger of such disturbances, so it is important that he should be properly instituted.

The controls are operators, who work sometimes in control, sometimes not, sometimes blending as a group. With some mediums, only controls, or only one control, is apparent in the work.

The controls must be under direction, or chaos will result. They are responsible for the physical, mental and spiritual reactions of the medium, and it behoves them to be adept in the management of these functions. Suppose a control of inferior intellect were to control continually, mental deterioration of the medium would set in. If anyone were allowed to control too long, or too often, or if anyone depraved were admitted, detriment would occur to the medium. The avenues of control must be guarded, and it is in the guide's hands who is allowed to approach.

When the guide himself operates as a control, he has to depend on others to do this work for him. There must, therefore, be a group composed of people who can be trusted to do the work assigned to them. Characteristically, they must have something which is blendable, so that together they make a perfect whole. They must be alert, intelligent, and prompted by spiritual desire and spiritual awareness. They must blend and link with one another, and with the guide and the medium. When the group is working, harmonising and synchronising, were one member to fail, the whole might be fraught with danger to guide, controls and medium.

We use complements of one another all the time to make the best whole. Various qualities are necessary for particular moments at work. Emotional stress must be balanced, dullness of sitters lightened, thoughts of sitters combated, desire of sitters for a particular thing guarded against.

The medium must also be watched, and all points of contact in the brain centres must be under control. The correct degree of trance must be maintained, and care taken that emotion neither depresses, nor exhilarates the medium too much. Her consciousness must be directed towards synchronising with awakening, so that it is easy and natural.

In the initial stages of development, use may be made of people who are not guides or skilled controls. No mediumship is worthwhile if it remains at this stage. There should be continual change of controls, until the group is established and the guide is in charge. Mediumship, especially mental mediumship, should be consistently progressive, or it will become automatic and repetitive. If a guide is directing, it will be progressive. It is, of course, quite possible the guide who directs the work does not function in control as I do.

If the medium is in too big a hurry to display her powers, the development is stopped and the controls are in command of something unfinished. The mediumship stays like a bridge partially built, the span not complete, so that it is impossible for communicators to pass to and fro, in comfort and happiness.

Imagine ropes and tackle used in haste: misdirection and accidents when the rope breaks. The bridge must be firmly and soundly built. There must be a director to keep it in order and a custodian to see to the safety of passengers crossing.

In the beginning, the medium should be under experts on both sides. There must be no dominating desires, and there must be confidence in the controls. There must therefore be an effort to produce evidence to establish in the sitters' minds that the controls know their business.

In time, it may happen that the medium comes into contact with people of strong ideas. If the guide is not yet established, and the medium is influenced by these sitters, their ideas will colour and influence the work of the controls. It is the duty of the circle to watch the development carefully and to guard against such influence. In friendly understanding they must help the medium over difficulties by creating harmony, truth and confidence.

Any person developing mediumship should receive love and care. The sitter is as important to the spirits operating as the medium is. We depend on your love, guidance and integrity. Your thoughts should be: 'Let me give my time so that those I know may make spiritual contact with my mind and spirit.' No one out of harmony should be allowed to sit.

If you think you have latent psychic powers and wish to develop them, sit for three months with a few friends. Give indication of your readiness to discover these powers. Your wish will be noted and help given. Have a quiet, pleasant evening, even if you only talk, but don't be erratic. On no account disturb your latent possibilities unless you realise the responsibility and are seeking, not exciting powers, but an opening for useful service. It is no easy path, but a serious undertaking.

Psychometry is the art of sensing an object. Suppose a piece of wood has been buried for centuries and is given to each of you in turn to hold. If anyone can sense and define the conditions of change that wood has gone through, then he has the makings of a medium. He becomes one with the article, gives it colour and form, lends himself to it, defines and makes clear the stages through which it has passed. That is the basis of all mediumship.

You may sit for long and nothing may happen, but if the stuff of mediumship is there, it will soon become malleable and quicken. What kind of medium you become depends upon expediency, on how best you can be used, and on your own desires. It is wrong to say you want to develop this or that type of mediumship, for that sets your mind in a groove. You must first become aware of your ability to sense things and learn how to apply it.

Mediumship should be watched and noted in its early stages. It needs no specific study by the medium, and indeed, it is better if she does not study it. If she is fortunate in sitters, who are constant through the years, they will learn much. It is they who are the students of the particular mediumship, and on them lies the special duty of observing all that is said and done. They must note reactions in the medium and in themselves, the feelings, hopes, fears and joys. If greater note were taken of the reactions of the sitters to the medium, and of the medium to the sitters, a better and finer mediumship would follow.

Harmony must be engendered in the circle, but never collusion or pacification, or lack of watchfulness and criticism. If the medium is sensible, she will trust the judgement of the sitters if they have proved intelligent, and take note of any discrepancies which arise. Every sitter has a responsibility towards the mediumship.

Judgement should be tempered with good breeding and taste, kindliness and good humour, as well as criticism.

All mediums are different, but certain conditions are unalterable. Some people suggest that certain rules should be laid down for developing circles, but this would lead the medium into a groove. False philosophies would creep in, certain things would be expected to happen, and this would delay or prevent the arrival of the guide, the spirit who should direct the work.

Age is a factor in the development of mediumship. The years of puberty are important, but it is unwise to develop at that time. The mediumship usually runs for a little, then stops. In any case, young people should not be asked to give up all other interests, for it is of no use to have mediumship as a part-time amusement.

Mediumship must be developed thoroughly so that the medium is master of the psychic power and can control its occurrence. If you are serious in development, you will find that it encroaches on normal work, so young people should not develop, unless mediumship is to be their life work. They should rather be taught to understand psychic power, shown how to lessen impulses and divert the power into useful channels. Then, when the quieter years come, it is quite possible mediumship may develop.

The next period, from the age of thirty-four to forty-eight, is the best time to develop, but conditions of life today are not favourable. A woman of that age will probably have children, but should have passed her busiest years with them. A man has married by then, however, and may have a family to support. It is not right to make mediumship a profession until groups of people take on the financial responsibilities of mediums, and let them rest in quiescent periods.

Some people think that desire opens the way to mediumship. It doesn't, unless there is the quality of psychic awareness. Other people think the power of mediumship is bestowed by spirits. They say: 'Why do the spirits not choose people of superior character and good education?'

Mediumship is a subtle something belonging to individuals born with it. All people are psychic, but not all have the power to develop mediumship. Of those who do develop, some are good, some mediocre, some indifferent, some bad. Similarly, in the arts you get the genius, the infant prodigy, those who show talent, but produce no masterpieces, and those who, from egoism, consider their own display excellent beyond dispute, however poor it may be.

In the arts, however, anyone can acquire certain techniques, but in mediumship it is different. It requires certain qualities of a personal nature, and a willingness to yield those propensities to competent people, unknown people, who will wield the power, and produce what is known as mediumship. This is difficult, especially if the medium is intelligent and unwilling, rightly, to yield even one hundredth part of herself to another. The growth is slow. It needs careful culture and conditions which are suited to it.

Fully developed mediumship is rare. The conditions are inherited, there when the person is born, but it may be that she never becomes a medium. The mediumship has to wait for the right moment to light it up. The guide is not the arbiter of the medium's fate, nor of anyone else's, and he must wait till she is ready. The medium is first a human being. Her character, personality, understanding and education are all part and parcel of her mediumship. We use her powers, blended and heightened by the group.

7

CONTROLS

Notes by Harriet McIndoe

In the home circle, we sitters were privileged to know, and to know as friends, the various members of the group who spoke to us. Their personalities were quite distinct from one another so that, without being told, we often knew who was speaking, although he would be using Mrs Thomson's voice in its ordinary tones.

We became aware of their comradeship and reliance upon one another, and their dedication to the work they had undertaken; how they complemented one another, each finding his own niche and acting with the others for the greater strength and efficacy of the whole. Gradually too we realised their reverence for P'shanta, and their devotion to him, whose disciples they were, their first care being to protect him from anything that could sully or demean. From them we too learned to value him truly.

In time, we realised that behind the scenes, not known to us, there were a great many other members of the group whose work was just as important to the success of the mediumship as that of the known controls. Some of these were contemporary with our friends, but others were of older generations. Occasionally we had a visit from one of these older spirits, messengers bringing us greetings or reassurance, sometimes admonition.

All, from the known members of the group to the messengers, were members of a very much larger group of people called the Torchbearers, who were dedicated to the service of mankind. Their work was widespread, and in many spheres, of which mediumship was only one.

P'shanta introduces the Torchbearers

It is quite wrong to imagine that the people of our world are unanimous in their view of life, its creation, philosophies, arts, and so on. There are many different ideas and schools of thought, and one such is a very large school called: the Torchbearers. The word 'school' is used in its original sense. It is not a building, but a school of thought, a body of people who are desirous of getting the best from life, joy, companionship, culture, learning: of giving service and of promoting the welfare of the whole community.

Most people on earth who have held a torch (musicians, artists, poets, all who have served their fellows selflessly, and those who attempted to save man from himself), work still for the development of mankind, both on earth and in Spirit. Such people gravitate towards the Torchbearers. Its teachings involve simply the acceptance of the normal laws of life. They hold no belief for the unknown; their brief is for the known and not to worship the unknown. They tell you to look to the known; do not serve the unseen; serve the seen; serve your fellows that are seen by you; and do not worry about gods you cannot see.

They incorporate in their lives the philosophy that goodness is God. They have no truck with the doctrinaire side of life, but believe in active service. Under the auspices of their school, there are many groups giving different types of service. There are artists and musicians, teachers and healers. Many go into physical conditions to succour prisoners, the poor and the sick. Passing from the earth does not debar spirits from living within the bounds of earth life. There is a continual coming and going of spirits among men. The short term of life on earth is insufficient to give the soul its full experience, and growth continues until the rightness of one's living is assured.

There is a band of sisters who work for suffering humanity. They frequent hospitals and institutions, homes and hovels, wherever expert guidance and treatment is needed, and they are at hand when death occurs. They go to the far corners of the earth to help those who are lonely or afraid. During air raids in all countries they work, capable, selfless, losing themselves in service to others. From their experience, they cull much. They desire to know why such vile conditions exist, and so they learn the sorry story of humanity. They see the courage and fineness of people bereft, and so gain strength to go on to braver and finer things. They seek no reward but that of having given a little ease, a little happiness.

Service on earth is in no way to their detriment. Many experiences can only come by contact with people of flesh. Many spirit people of fine growth and development walk the earth among men with great enjoyment, and suffer no soiling. They have learned how to do that, and how to protect themselves and be inviolate. Only the less developed are soiled.

Others of the school are interested in problematic things, in the study of the sciences. What they learn, they try to pass on to you on earth, opening the way to man's greater knowledge. They watch for the moment when, in some mind, the dividing door will be opened, the union of two minds achieved, and the knowledge established.

Some brave souls there seek to influence bodies engaged in administrative work. This is difficult work in which success is very limited. Some set about making people feel at home when they arrive in the Spirit World, giving homely attentions, hospitality and so forth, so that happiness is spread and balance restored.

Each knows that what he cannot do, someone else can, and he is able to reach the one with greater knowledge. He has no sense of incompetence; it is a matter of pooling knowledge. There is also art, music and song, dancing, laughter and fun. There are societies for talks and debates, and temples of truth and worship, where all who are interested in the highest and best are able to seek fountains of understanding.

P'shanta talks about control during the development of mediumship

It is important to have a working band of spirits, like-minded and in harmony with one another, but with great individual differences, so that their different facets can fit into a perfect whole. Ideas can be put forward that are not the medium's, using words the medium would not use. The aim is to induce in the medium a passive state for the controls, and by degrees to make her conscious mind quiescent, so that what we say will not be altered into what the medium wishes, or thinks we ought to say. Not all mediums go through this phase, so not all are amenable to what the control wishes to say.

To continue the process, the control makes his approach, bringing his own emanation. The unconscious mind of the medium is dealt with after the conscious mind, entry of the control being finally made through the unconscious. His individuality is merged with the medium's, so a little of personality is lost. The medium's mind is not dormant.

Control is not made operable by one person alone. There are many forces in play, each doing its own part, and the particular response obeys its own stimuli. The impulse may come from afar, for vibration may carry a message many miles. It is very quick in coming, but slows down till the receptive brain of the medium picks it up.

Each medium has a different range. A fine instrument can reach out: it is more sensitive, quicker rays can operate. With another medium, they must come further and slow down and are therefore more disconnected. The quicker the control in vibration, the better the transmission.

The medium is the most important operator, and much depends on her integrity. Sitters expect returns, and if the medium's principles are not strong enough, she simply pleases the sitters. She endows their friends in Spirit with extraordinary qualities and powers instead of portraying them as essentially the same people as they were on earth, all to suit the sitters' preconceived ideas. The communicating spirit becomes bewildered at what he is purported to be saying, but he cannot stop or alter it.

Do not encourage those mediums who do not produce evidence. Do not use a channel which professes communication from spirits, and yet simply provides stimulus in the form of prophecy of good fortune, well-being and so on. Communication is the first and most important link between us. You must establish the facts which you claim, that personality survives death, and that the dead are able to communicate.

It is not advisable to merge completely. If control is absolute so that the mind of the medium is not used at all, the method is clumsy. Think of yourself as a body and mind. Your movements are automatic, but a baby has to learn to command its muscles. So, in absolute control, the control would have to learn to use the medium's muscles.

I, as guide, am always in charge of Mrs Thomson, and always in the field of operation. If I were to withdraw my influence, she would be open to intruders because she is a magnetised field. I am able to alter my consciousness and unconsciousness until they are in the same field as hers.

Distant control is done by rays of thought. There is no closeness and no merging. When in trance, her mind is in abeyance. Now that my own English is fluent, I do not use so much of her mind. I pause sometimes to get words which are not those she would readily use.

That in itself shows that it is not her mind in operation.

It must be made clear to you that it depends entirely upon the strength of control how much of the medium's mind is left active. That does not mean that the veridical value of communications is lessened by the activity of her mind. Transmission may be a little distorted, words altered, perhaps, but not much, the sense remains. We have so often used Mrs Thomson actively, that we trust the action of her mind without a great deal of control. The impression made on the medium's mind is dependent on the personality behind it. Sometimes it can't be made strong; sometimes sitters interfere.

The medium is still the medium. Mrs Thomson is still Mrs Thomson, whether she is controlled or not. She still controls her body, although apart from it. She senses the attitude of the sitter. She is sensitive when in trance. For example, if a door bangs, she jumps and then she feels ill.

Some sitters say: 'How far away does Mrs Thomson go when she is in trance?' She could go a thousand miles away, but she would still be securely linked to her body. If she were not, she wouldn't come back.

Mrs Thomson hears me when I talk. She doesn't know that, for she doesn't remember. Because she is determined to have nothing to do with the actual communication, we work well. Her fault is that she censors us, but she does not change the sense of what is said. Of course, there is one great advantage in that. She censors, consciously or unconsciously, the unconventional things that might be said. I am not always sure what you people might take exception to. It is only when I get the sense of a thing that I understand what is meant. I am only beginning to realise that all things should not be taken literally. It is very useful to be able to depend upon the sense of decorum of the medium.

From the beginning I determined to become fluent in English, for if I had not, Mrs Thomson would have become fidgety and spoiled our work. I studied so that I might lessen my impress upon her and so establish a working partnership. When tranced, she makes a splendid link for us. I'm not sure but that consciously she might be just as good, but she lacks confidence. The trance state suits her better.

There is great need to show mediums that how they live, their personality, their habits, and so on, can all go to bring greater perfection to their mediumship. All the childish chattering and inane talk and so on, which one sometimes hears through certain mediums, and which is accredited to spirits, is aided by the mediums. All that puerility is not becoming to spirits. We would have nothing of that. That is why it is good to have in a medium, submission, trust, and desire for the best. We also feel that a medium should develop their own personality and intelligence. Too much trance, too frequent, or too deep, has a dulling effect, so that mediums come to depend on minds other than their own.

People often ask if it's possible for us to talk on a subject which is outside the medium's knowledge: for example, a scientific subject, using the usual scientific and technical terms. The answer is: I think it might be possible, but it would be difficult. It would have to come by transmission, and it would come very slowly. In fact, we had to scold Mrs Thomson for doubting the possibility of such transmission. She seems to think that a control is limited by the intelligence and education of the medium. To a certain extent, this is so, but not entirely. I think it could be demonstrated that such a condition, as, for instance, lack of education, need not be a stumbling block.

If we speak about something Mrs Thomson has read, that registers. The process is so quick that it reaches her mind before she has spoken. Sometimes what we say is inhibited because she is so anxious not to influence what is said that what she knows is omitted. She hears what we say before it is uttered by herself and may be most rebellious. There is too a resentment against things of which she is aware coming through as evidence. She used to try to interfere, saying: 'Don't say that, it isn't evidence.'

She can approve too; sometimes she says: 'Clever piece of evidence, that.' She is a spirit working with us. All her intelligence and abilities are heightened. When she is quiescent and when we can keep her occupied while in trance, everything is easy; but if there is anything controversial, particularly if it has been discussed in her hearing, the words may stop. But we have never suffered from substitution by her.

We are using a mind which is docile, dominant, strong, weak, and so on at different times. It is never twice the same. A control has many things to do while working. He must be prepared for, and be aware of changes in the trance state, and many other things. It would probably amaze you to learn what capabilities are required of a control. The act of communication is not brought about without much planning and effort.

P'shanta introduces his group members (the controls): Raymond, Julian, Rupert, David and Silver Pine

My own particular group are concerned with work that takes them among earth people. They are men of intelligence and integrity. They felt the need to do something of service to humanity during the time they would have lived on earth. They have turns of duty in group work not connected with mediumship. Many are still interested in the profession they chose, so they help those who follow it on earth. They must choose someone with whom they can be happy, and they must be skilled in their profession so that they can help. If they are barristers, they must work in worthy causes. A doctor will cooperate with doctors on earth.

Raymond

It is a fallacy to believe that during trance the medium enters the control's etheric body, in the same way as the control enters the medium's physical body to facilitate communication. We never do that. That is quite an erroneous idea. There is, if you like, a certain extra body which surrounds Mrs Thomson, and is a field which we enter.

She does not enter our etheric bodies, but she does enter our etheric field. A certain development had to be completed before P'shanta could enter her field, and she, his. I should be rash to generalise about mediumship, for every medium is a law to himself. I can speak only about the means and methods in which we have specialised, and which we have built up.

When I speak through Mrs Thomson as a communicator, as distinct from a control, I do not think at all about the mechanism. If I did, I'd lose control immediately. This evening, I am control as well as communicator. It is a long time since I controlled like this, so I am finding it difficult. When I forget the mechanism and become comfortable, and feel as if I'm talking normally, then I talk easily.

Ordinary communicators have nothing to do with controlling. If you send a telegram, you write words and sign your name without thinking of the means of transmission. You leave that to the specialists. So, it is with regularised lines of communication, that is, with properly developed mediums. It is the skilled assistants who see that the communicator does communicate.

My particular job is to make the medium ready for control. I must dull the particular nerve centres not required. Sight must be shut out. Hearing is a sense we use, so it must be quickened and heightened. Speech must be kept active. Other conditions which are of no use to us, for example, the medium's active mind, are made quiescent.

The medium in trance must be looked after so that she does not begin to be active. It is also very important that she does not go into a cataleptic condition for that would endanger her health, so we must see that her blood is kept flowing freely.

Julian

We sometimes obey instinct blindly as you do on earth, and are not aware of the forces guiding us. At other times we feel some power compelling us. Quite a few of us felt we were choosing what we did, but afterwards, when we had lost some conceit, we realised we had been led. Most of us have grown into our work.

In communication, we have to merge ourselves into the work, and all must be synchronised in harmony and tone, so that P'shanta can operate well. We work under his aegis, as his personal group, his bodyguard. Without him, we could do very little.

Most of us who have been connected with mediumship for a time, have been 'at school' to have the tutelage of P'shanta and other superior ones who link to that group. Most of us prepare for further adventure by serving an apprenticeship with him, undertaking the discipline of controlling oneself in any conditions and of being under the influence and example of P'shanta.

If one wants to undertake the mission, one must learn patience under any circumstances. The joy is in the fulfilment. When we speak of group work, we are not referring simply to mediumistic work, although that is a great part of it, because we have been chosen as the guardians of P'shanta.

P'shanta loses much of his identity in descending to physical conditions. We are in charge of the proceedings and must see that no harm comes to him, Mrs Thomson, or the communicator. We have to ward off those who would dogmatise, and we censor anything that might be said contrary to the ideology of the Torchbearers.

We serve P'shanta wherever he serves. Our first loyalty and duty are to him, although we are naturally interested in Mrs Thomson and the friends we make among you. Mrs Thomson has dedicated herself to her charge. She serves P'shanta as we do. You are well served because of this.

We have a great many duties and we have to go anywhere to perform the tasks we have taken upon ourselves. No one gives us a task. We think we have chosen, but we are guided towards it. We pass through certain stages of growth and initiation, and realise more and more the humbleness of our position, and how much schooling we need to lose the sense of our own importance. The most difficult lesson, which I have not yet fully mastered, is first to recognise oneself as an individual, and then to lose all sense of self.

All sorts of arts have to be learned, much must be undone, little mean things lost in acts of atonement. Atonement is beautiful when one has accomplished something to wipe out the fault. There is no big book of sins. Sins are personal, known within oneself. In trying to atone, one finds oneself something perfect and new, instead of soiled. We have many fine active organisations which give useful service. These are communities of friends who live in harmony together. They don't work because they must; they choose whom they want to work with and are therefore in the company of their friends.

Rupert

Many spirits remain in close contact with earth in order to help man. They influence men through their thoughts, but of course, the thoughts can be, and often are, shut out. There may be many people in Spirit who help you, quite unknown to yourself. For some reason they are attracted to you.

You can all get help if you ask for it. Think: 'Somewhere there is a power that can direct me. I must find that source so that it can help me to release my power.' That power can be used for evil as well as good. You must be analytical enough to decide if your prayer is for the best in the long run. Prayer can be selfish or selfless.

Help does not usually come when asked for, but rather when you are getting on with the job. You must do your own work and use your own initiative. It is most important to learn to do what you are doing thoroughly and well. Power and effort put out will knit you to conditions in Spirit similar to your own.

In the same way, people can direct their energies to degradation and focus their interest on dark things, and so there will be a fusion with those in Spirit with similar tastes. The law of attraction leads undeveloped spirits to their counterparts on earth, just as people of wisdom in Spirit are attracted to people of wisdom on earth. Fusion causes the direction of impulses.

Part of my work relates to trance. This consists of the submerging of the conscious mind to a sleep-like state and raising the unconscious mind. With Mrs Thomson, I am not responsible for the subjection of the conscious mind, which is the work of one highly skilled and experienced.

When that is done, it is comparatively easy to make links. I stand by and make ready to introduce separate entities. The whole process is now skilful and swift, but at the beginning, Mrs Thomson's mind was not practised in subjecting itself to the influence of another mind.

My first job was to make her mind pliable, and so mould it as to make it our own instrument. The clay has to be worked until it is malleable enough for a master to use. Until this state is reached it is not possible for a sitter to recognise the personality of a communicator, and much practice is needed to achieve it. Many impressions were made with Mrs Thomson by different methods. I had to enact different characters and watch both the reactions of Mrs Thomson and the sitters.

At first, Mrs Thomson's chief reaction was a slight exhilaration, a certain abnormality. As the unconscious is raised there must be exhilaration and a corresponding deflation afterwards. This calls for judicious treatment, for it could easily cause suffering. I have had a lot to learn and have been called to book many times. I have had to learn by my mistakes how to overcome my inadequacies, when to use corrective measures, how to stop conditions causing pain, and so on.

This sounds as though I have had to know all pathology. I have not, but I had wise advisers who could not themselves come into Mrs Thomson's psychic field, for she was not then sufficiently developed for their influence. There was a great deal of laboratory work. In one evening, eight or ten personalities of widely different types would be presented: a policeman, a singer, an explorer, and so on. Sometimes these were impersonations, sometimes actual people were brought.

At first, I found extrication of myself at the end of the sitting very difficult, and often had to await rescue. The more annoyed I got, the more I was dug in. To begin with, it was like having gas, almost as suffocating, and with the medium demanding my retreat. Our two minds were wrangling, trying to gain possession, now one on top, now the other. That is as it should be, because if the medium were subservient all the time it would be difficult for her when the control was released to come to a proper state.

There is so much carelessness about development that people who say that it leads to mental disturbance have a certain amount of justification. This is not because there are malicious spirits waiting to pounce, but because there is disturbance of mental equilibrium, excitement of the unconscious, and inability to adjust after depression. Psychic disturbance may be great, and there may be severe pain. Our medium felt that the nausea, pains and sleeplessness were too great, and that she ought to stop sitting. This phase, however, lasted only about three months.

In the next stage there was more response to the individual communicators and there was more evidence. The state of expectancy was good, and it kept us going. We knew now how much psychic force we had to use, but we had to find out the best form to use it in.

Gradually we began to exercise our privileges in a positive way. Things became more normal. We were able to control proceedings and there were fewer intrusions. Gradually a competent team was formed to deal with any disturbances. Until the development is well forward, there may be intrusion at any time.

We had to debate various subjects with the sitters to get flexibility of mind, quickness, exchange of repartee, sequence of wording. We had to watch for 'colouring', that is, the temperament or characteristics of one control being left with the medium so that it affected the personality of the next. We had to guard against our own efforts colouring or blotting out communications which we might be passing on, lest we cause distortion, perhaps obliteration, of the personality of the true communicator.

When a certain stage was reached, the guide, P'shanta, was introduced. By then we were sure that under normal conditions the work would be productive. There was uninterrupted vocal activity, the words coming out just as if the medium were using the apparatus herself. Thoughts from outside were cut off, and we could see that the medium's conscious mind did not come to the surface while we were operating.

In trance speaking from the public platform, or to groups of people, the control is the chief operator. The medium must be shut out, and the control be the sole mind operating before we get accurate and concise wording of thoughts. As a consequence, the medium's mind is in submission, the brain suffers strain, and depression or exhilaration results, dependent on circumstances such as the interest of the audience.

Minor things contribute, so the audience should be warm and comfortable, and there should be no disturbance or distractions. All these things have an effect on the medium afterwards, and determine whether she will be depressed and dull or excitedly happy. The responsibility for results lies on the circle or audience.

Critics who say that as a result of development, a medium has no mind of her own, talk nonsense. If you were psychic enough to attract other entities, and if you continued without supervision, you would find that you had no mind of your own, no personality, lack of desire to waken to life, and might finally reach a state of idiocy.

It is fairly easy in a circle for someone discarnate to merge in the mesh-like structure of the psychic, and give semblance of control, but emergence from it is another matter. The spirit who becomes enmeshed is not usually malicious, but merely ignorant of what he is doing. He has got himself into the position of being unable to extricate himself from the potential medium, with consequent distress to both.

One can develop many things alone in the quietness, but not mediumship. To try to do so is dangerous. It needs a circle, and in the early stages, the medium is as dependent on the sitters as on the controls. It is interesting to watch the effect of the sitters on the unconscious mind of the medium. We have to be sure that the medium is not too amenable to the influence of the sitters. We do, however, make use of the sitters' minds and their possibilities in positive ways.

David

I am convinced that throughout my life on earth and in Spirit, guiding influences have attended me, of which, I know nothing at all. Is it possible to acknowledge such influences and still retain a sane perspective, and know that one cannot receive guidance unless one is more or less unaware of it?

Your relatives and friends do their best to help you, but their power is not great enough to apply those laws which guide, comfort and console you. There is great power, manifested through many channels, which distributes this vital force, stirring up the best in people, cultivating the desire for good. Think of the fine people of the past who have held high the torch of the persistence of good, which is in itself, a beacon to all.

This power of good reached us prior to our birth. It is an inspiration from our ancestors, from all those who have sought to do good, who would bear anything to further a cause. All these people are part of some greater thing which, hovering over us, gives of itself to us, guiding, influencing, inspiring us. It is, perhaps, not so dramatic to think of guidance in that way. People prefer to think of a particular person guiding and helping them. But I am talking of greater things, great impulses, great inspiration to do one's best without questioning why one is forced forward.

A beam of light is directed on people in both worlds, so that they may become instruments for powers operating on a wider field. These powers have knowledge that we could be of use under their indirect influence. They leave us free scope for our own development but draw us towards this ray, which rotates fanwise over all who can feel its influence. Gradually we converge with others who are drawn by it, so that the greater number of units merge into a perfect whole.

Great patience belongs to these powers. The person who is the centre of attention often stubbornly refuses to be persuaded or guided, and many years may pass before he will act in accord with directed thought. No one can command anyone to give up his active life to the influence of another. Gentle persuasion and watchfulness for the correct moment are all necessary.

The true source of all good is far off, but we all have the power to absorb what we need of it by prayer and meditation. We, in Spirit, learn that. We find a power is directed to us; we receive a call. It is as intangible to us as it is to you, as if it gently persuaded us into certain circumstances which have a direct bearing on our lives.

Silver Pine: control and healer

Most people think that when their friends are dead, they immediately become happy and well. The majority of people, however, have to make many adjustments before they find real happiness. Health and happiness with us are synonymous. You have heard of healing places in the Spirit World, hospitals as you would say. I have in my care such a place, where I gather together those skilled in the art of readjustment. Some people are naturally skilled in this work, but most have to be trained very carefully for it.

Many young men and women gladly surrender themselves to the work of healing. They desire to serve. No one is refused the chance to learn what such service involves. There are many tests that they must pass without knowing that they are tests. They must have endurance, sympathy, love, truth, foresight and a sense of humour. They must be compassionate, though just, and above all things, they must have that resilience of spirit which can never be bowed down.

Very few pass these tests immediately, so training must be undergone by those who desire to work in our centres. They must themselves be readjusted. The first principle is renunciation. They are stripped of all preconceived ideas of their own worth. The pure soul stands ready to acquire and learn anew. As they progress, they become naturally joyous, buoyant spirits. They have learned true happiness, expressive happiness.

Each helper must understand the basic principles underlying health, and I do not speak here of physical health. They must study psychology. They must understand why 'self' desires certain things, and the responses to stimuli and colour. Such understanding is acquired only gradually.

You may be imagining a large institution with beds, doctors and nurses. Such is not the case. My own particular theory is that reconstruction, to be effective, must be begun on the right lines, so I never permit the carrying over of an illusion, or a desire on the patient's part to hold fast to a state of invalidism.

Our methods are quite different from yours, although even among you there are some clinics where adjustments are made through surroundings. Colour and natural influences help the individual to adjust to the normal. The conditions of restoration are available on earth as in Spirit. They depend entirely on the individual patient, and that is why an understanding of psychology is so necessary.

A helper is of little value if he cannot analyse the condition of the patient by glance, by contact, and through talking with him, and so decide the attention that is needed. We know that only certain people can help certain others, so the person best fitted to give help is drawn to the one who needs it.

Some people are brought to our notice before their deaths by friends, either on earth, or in Spirit, who apply to us for help. We prefer to link with people before death to give us power to bring them under our influence, so that they waken into surroundings already prepared.

Colour, breezes, and spiritual influence play upon them, and bring about once more the desire to live, and to live in health. That such preparations are necessary is to many people a shock because of the old idea of transformation on death, but the only transformation is brought about by gradual change.

Many people adjust themselves to their new life very quickly. Mentally bright people are the quickest to respond. Those who are suspicious, even of the conditions into which we put much love, are very difficult to help. When faced with love they become afraid of themselves, as well as of those who shower it on them. Many people are afraid to enter the conditions which would bring out the best in them, and so they live an abnormal life.

I wish you could come with me to the various places we have. In some, insane people are treated. We induce a state of complete passivity. This is necessary so that we can begin the process of re-education from the start. A deep sleep, or trance state, supervenes. It is not hypnotic. There is a gradual awakening. Then there is a series of small glass-like houses where, in a partly conscious state, the mind is learning to be alone with itself. Further on, you would see attendants speaking to the patient and making suggestions. Later you would see him walking in the gardens, doing a little easy work.

On earth, doctors must certify a person insane and then he is bundled away into an institution. In the Spirit World, relatives of a new arrival often have some such difficulties to deal with, but the problem is not necessarily insanity as it is known on earth. Many things give alarm in Spirit, which are not even considered eccentric on earth.

The family is an integral part of man's relationships, and the family still holds good in Spirit. When people arrive, they make union again with their relatives. In some instances, these relatives may find difficulties arising. The strange behaviour of a newcomer may startle them. They will approach an elder among them and ask him to speak to the recalcitrant one, who resents that. He thinks them old-fashioned. After all, they've been a long time dead.

Sometimes the family asks us to help. We try to persuade the newcomer that there is something a little wrong, and by psychological methods we get him to accept our ministrations for a period. We gather together those who really are mentally ill; those with brains undeveloped since childhood; those who are eccentric; and those who think themselves very important.

Even ordinary people find it very difficult to get into the smallness of the real self. Most of these have to be willing patients. Nothing is applied that would make them feel uncomfortable. Even the 'most important people' are treated as they feel they should be treated. We all go round being very important together. We mix people carefully, so that like meets like. Important people have to deal with important people, so that the meek and mild are not imposed upon. It's all so natural that the individual doesn't realise what has happened. He's often not aware that he's receiving any special treatment.

There are people who have hoarded money, left it hidden somewhere, been suspicious of banks and neighbours, gone in rags, picked up cigarette ends. These misers are in a doleful state if they have no money, so we manufacture money. By making conditions alike for all of them, we take away competition. The miser gradually realises that there is no need to be afraid, but he is still suspicious; and hides his money from his neighbours. As adjustment begins, free access is made possible to all that he needs, and there is no longer any incentive to keep on hoarding.

The miracle begins when he wants to give something away. At first, he does not give, but furtively puts things away from him. Then he actually gives something away, but finds that the recipient has no use for it. It is not really a gift, for it is something he does not want and is trying to get rid of it.

We try to woo him from self-centredness by surrounding him with things that he covets. By beauty and love and laughter we wake him to the knowledge that the world is a very beautiful place, and that the eye must look outwards to perceive beauty; that possessions as such mean nothing; that true satisfaction comes from understanding spiritual things; and that no virtue accrues from giving but the sheer joy of sharing with another. When an individual possesses nothing, and is ready to go out to give and to create, he is cured.

I have been told that there is an idea abroad that in Spirit there are large institutions or hospitals, where sisters of mercy bring people from lower regions, from hell. This probably comes from attempts to translate ideas into words. It is difficult to give you the picture as it is. It probably came through mediums by mental impact, which is not close enough for true translation.

People who eschew trance and control know very little of the fineness necessary to be in rapport with refined spirits. The interpretation of the thought impulse is therefore couched by the medium in his own language and ideas. Hence the picture of hell according to Mephistophelian fables.

I'd like to paint a brighter picture of sunny vales and hills and grassy places: of trees and flowers and children, of love and companionship; and of attendants who adopt the role most suited to the environment of the patient.

Silver Pine reviews the advancement of man

There is always some different angle presented to those who watch the story of man's development. Many pictures unfold in glowing colours. There are some dark places, many unhappy spots and many mistakes, but happiness gilds the pages, and the colour is life, and the fire consumes that which is unworthy.

The book of life is a great volume. It is your privilege to read the pages of the past, and to be actors in the page that will be written tomorrow. In the future, you will read your page, and see in it much that is in the pages of the past.

You will see your folly and your wisdom, your littleness and your greatness; how you spurned guidance and disdained knowledge; how light came to you and you darkened your windows against it. As the page turns and you can read no more, you will know that onwards you go to the clean pages, where there is nothing spoiled, nothing beautified. That is the promise of life.

Men, through all time, have been divided into sections, different races and different civilisations. Some make great contributions to the advancement of man; some show a tendency to reversion. Men, through all the ages, have desired to know the reason for life.

Different nations have sought to answer by the method of appeasement. They attempt to quieten the questioner in order to frustrate new endeavour. Penance is laid on those who, having seen a little light, try to make it easier for their fellows. Many advancements have died ere they were born, and so continues the mystery.

Today it is even greater. Most people are mystified at the conduct of life: its cruelty and its waste; its incoherence and lack of cohesion. Instead of becoming enlightened, man becomes benighted. Life seems to hem him in rather than to open the gate to freedom. Is there no way of understanding? Must escape through death be the only way to the freshness of a new dawn? Has truth become falsified? Have we been denied the understanding that would give true enlightenment? Is man just a whim of someone greater than himself? The problem of man's life is indeed a story stranger than any story conceived by the brain. Let us see if we can find some little path through the great forest of darkness and fear.

Today you lead lives that are far removed from natural conditions of living. Is it right to claim that man in the past was fitter to perceive truth than he is today? Or, is man of today the superior? In my own time, man lived simply. In the great wide country of my birth, man lived surrounded by unspoiled nature. In these wide spaces, nature performed her miracles unspoiled.

Nature sometimes overproduced, and if greater than man's needs, he left it. For house and clothing, he had skins, decorated by the art of those who could conceive the pattern and make the colour. His needs were his cooking pot, his spears and his arrows. In so simple an existence, was man denied happiness? He could see the countless stars and the wide face of the heavens, and try to trace the thoughts that found birth within him: and he could enjoy the warmth of friendship.

Man has expanded and built for himself cities; he has sought leisure and developed the powers within him. He has expressed his words in print, and transmitted his thoughts into colours on canvas. He prides himself on his increasing greatness and power over all the earth.

But has he, his birthright, happiness, within his grasp? Does he hold the secret of life? Does he rule the earth? Whether now, or in the past life, is he still the same?

Man looks forward, over to a new knowing, to know his destiny. But all through physical life, the same conditions that thwart him have been in existence. He, the essential self, has remained unaltered. As one age succeeds another, each race boasts that it is the super race. Is this true? Are you more greatly blessed than I? Can you love, laugh and live better than I did? Is it my privilege to have caught up with you?

Life becomes more pressing, and therefore, more mysterious to this age of machinery. Something has gone wrong, if each successive age has failed to find the great truths and the enlightenment which should come from them. These ages have failed to make their land happy, a place where children can find good will. As we look back with the historian, we find him pitying each race before him, forgetting their contribution to the continuity of life.

Life is like a great river: divided into many small channels, wandering and twisting, but all eventually uniting in one great flow. Many times, man has thought he has come to a great breakup, to the end of the world. The swirl of the mighty torrent swept him over the precipice, and yet, once over, he came to a still pool.

We, in America, had leisure. We were able to pursue life more quietly. We could ponder over the greatness and littleness of life, and think of the spirit that broods over all things. We saw that there was no stilling of life. We knew that far into the future would go men and women charged with the development of many things. They would pursue life as we did.

Some of us were shaken by the knowledge that an era was closing. We trembled for those who would hold so great a burden. We swore to watch how they bore and how they delivered it, and so we still do. Still, we watch and succour and play our part. That makes us brothers of one great heritage.

As man developed, he devised implements and treasures for himself. As he built, his need to protect grew the greater, and his implement of protection changed. He defended himself from those who could wrest from his grasp what he had gained.

As man's possessions increased, so he became covetous. Today it is easily seen that man has followed that tendency. Once again, he is on the brink of the precipice. As he is forced onwards to he knows not what, it is still that which he possesses that he fears most to lose. He has been taught that only material things count. He cannot understand that even if he was alone and without possessions, he would still find the essentials of living.

The story will yet be written of how man, forced by the river of life, fell from the height of the precipice and found himself in the eddies of a stilling pool. Right through the ages, there is a repetition, which, with each repetition, becomes more and more fantastic, for man, while he has increased his possessions, has forgotten to increase the all-knowing part that speaks of wisdom. Why should man seek to destroy himself to make life more lasting? He is scarcely wiser now than in his beginning.

Man in his folly and greed has produced much that speaks only of safety, well-being and wealth. He has made a fetish of something and worships it. He no longer seeks spirit in earth, sea and sky. Man is too harassed to live. He is scorched by the glint of his golden god.

Is there anything that can release man from his folly: anything that will make him hearken to the voices that say he can only be guided by his own instinct?

The earth will give always to man, but even earth will not produce when man is foolish enough to destroy the necessary elements. So, the spiritual forces of life cannot glisten and shine on man when he destroys the essentials of spirit living.

You have been told again and again the errors you commit as a race. You cannot shut out the harshness and discordances, unless you have the key to take you beyond the barrier, and enter the places of true living. Men must do, as we do in Spirit, nurse people back to a newer realisation, cause life to spring afresh, show their fellows a truer path.

Man has had pioneers to point the way. Rarely do they, while in flesh, see those pointers utilised. It is left to others to mould the teachings. These forget to seek whence the knowledge came, and have spoiled its growth. Man must go back a little. He must stand back and see what he has created. Make your instruments of destruction only to destroy what would destroy you. Be not slaves to your gods. Grow in stature and grace. Each successive age will learn from the past. Be assured that man will pass this phase. You will still have the chance to gain happiness, but only through attempts to make it for yourself and others in the simple things.

P'shanta, the guide, gives advice to the controls

Before linking, controls must ensure that all apertures are shut and that there is no intrusion. Lines of light must be maintained between the controls and the medium to ensure uninterrupted transfusion of light between control and medium. Breaks should not occur if everything is joined up.

Controls should be prepared for every eventuality with the sitters because they (sitters) are inconsistent and unpredictable. Prepare against the unexpected. The line of link must be remembered. Lines of thought should be carefully controlled. Attention must be paid to those communicators who are less able to stand apart, and any mention of undesirable subjects is prohibited.

Speech is important. It must be modulated. There should be no more colouring of any communication than what is required. The individualities of the communicators should be carefully observed, but the controls should control the communicators, not the other way round.

8

COMMUNICATORS

From time to time, different communicators spoke to members of the Circle of the Open Door through the trance mediumship of Mrs Edith Thomson.

An elderly man gives an account of his passing

Where did I get off? Oh yes, back in the hospital. I think it got kind of dark. Then I saw faces I knew: my mother, my father and many others. I got glimpses of them, backwards and forwards. So many voices and faces were mixed I couldn't get anyone in particular.

I didn't suffer anything. I believe I had a bit of pain in the back. I can remember sighing. Someone gave me some water. Then I felt myself floating, just like it is when you dream you are floating on air. I couldn't stand. I tried and fell back. I kept on floating. I clearly remember thinking: 'You'll look stupid floating about like this.' Then I tried to straighten up, but I fell back again.

And then I clearly saw myself. I certainly got a fright. I began sweating. I said: 'I'm a goner,' and I tried to straighten again. I heard a click in my head, and jings, I straightened up. I started to go forward, but I was cloudy in my mind and everything seemed foggy. I thought: 'If I'm dead, where am I going? I can't see.' It took me a little time to see. I couldn't stand still. I seemed to be moving under someone else's power, just like floating on air.

After I'd floated about a bit, I heard people call to me. I said: 'Who is it? Speak a little louder.' I clearly got a word or two I recognised, and the mist began to clear and it was just like a summer's day, not hot or cold, just nice. I thought: 'This is good. I'm getting out of the mist.'

I thought I must be going to heaven, but it didn't come up to the stories. I didn't hear a trumpet or anything. The people whose voices I heard, I thought I'd see soon. But on I went and the voices followed me.

But I got through the mist and then I saw someone in white. That gave me a scare. But he was jolly and kind: a sentry, I think. I've never found out who he was. He said: 'Come along with me. Your name is Tom.'

I said: 'Yes, how did you know?'

'Oh,' he said, 'We know you. I've got a bed for you.'

'Oh,' I thought. 'Out of one bed, into another.'

So, he took me along to a bed and there I saw my mother right beside it. In I went, and they said I slept for a fortnight. When I awoke, I stretched myself and said: 'Now I'll be getting back home and Mary won't need to worry anymore.'

Then it came back to me, and I called out, and the person in white came in. 'You're dead, you know,' he said.

'Yes,' I said. 'I thought so.'

'This is your home now,' he told me. 'And you will just have to face the situation. Everything will be all right.'

And then I saw the rest of them. It was a little overwhelming at first. Then I saw that I was in a city, at least, I suppose you would call it that. All sorts of people were there. I thought: 'I'm going to like this place.' But I forgot to tell you. I don't know how it happened, but I was at my own funeral.

A young musician does not know he has died

Occasionally, someone who has died fails to realise that he is dead. He may remain for some time in a confused state, unable to make contact with people on earth, and refusing to acknowledge spirit entities whom he may regard as hallucinations. He can sometimes be helped by speaking through a medium, for he recognises that the sitters are alive, and if he will talk to them, he may gradually become aware of his true condition. One such, was a young musician.

On this occasion, Mrs Thomson had a strong desire to hear music just before she went into trance, and several records were played. She showed signs of distress. Someone asked for water. Thinking it was Mrs Thomson who wanted it, a sitter rose, thereby breaking the trance. P'shanta took charge and told us he was trying to bring in a young musician who had suffered greatly.

'I want water! Why do you torment me? I'm not dead. I'm alive. No one can thrust it down my throat that I'm dead. I must live to make music. I'm not afraid to die. I would have fought, but they wouldn't let me. They shut me up. I'm not dead, I'm alive. Music can never die.'

'Neither can you,' said a sitter. 'You are music.'

'Music: I? No, I just catch a strain from the infinite. All I desire.'

'What interrupted your making of music?' said another sitter.

'Violence, war: and what is being done about it.'

'The United Nations?' said the first sitter.

'Pft!' said the musician. 'Very little can be done against such evil.'

'We are trying to do a little by being here for you,' responded the first sitter. 'Do you know where you are?'

'I'm in hell, but I'm not dead. I've been moved about so much. Where am I now?'

'Glasgow, Scotland,' said the other sitter.

'I can't believe it.'

'Don't you recognise a Scottish voice?' continued the sitter.

'Yes, I did think I heard a Scottish voice. I like the homely, friendly people of Scotland. But it's not Glasgow I want to be in. It's Sutherland.'

'That's in Scotland, too,' said a third sitter.

'I am not quite ignorant of the geography of the British Isles,' commented the musician. Someone laughed. 'It sounds good to hear laughter again. Let's talk and talk about music, about life, about everything. Do you remember what Shelley wrote? *Music, when soft voices die, vibrates in the memory.* Isn't it beautiful? Beauty to me is life. I do want to live. Have you ever known what it is to hope, and go on hoping and always have it dashed?'

The sitters then told the musician that others had been in a similar position and had made their way out of it.

'No one has suffered as I have. They beat me. No one has suffered as I did.'

'Are you ready to take the opportunity if it does come,' continued the sitters, 'to live again and make music?'

'If I could believe it I would! I can't die. I must make music. There's something I must say. I begin to feel that pain in my head again. Why am I feeling that pain in my head again?'

'That is life returning,' said a sitter.

'Life, yes, I want to live. I'll stand the pain in my head if I live. If there's anything after death, surely it would be different from this. I'm numb. I feel a little pain. I've been numb so long. Why should I be so numb?'

'I think you've suffered so much, that you've shut yourself up in suffering,' said a sitter.

'That's it! Shut myself in suffering so that I feel nothing. I grew numb. I had to go on living. It was hell, but I was alive. Oh, to keep alive! I remember Scotland, beautiful Scotland, lovely Scotland, homely people, worthy people, kindly people, rugged like the hills. Give me life so that I can live.'

The musician then talked of the things that he loved and of his desire to make music. 'I see a green valley: green. I haven't seen anything green for so long. There's water there, water! It looks as if it were the Tweed. It might be the Avon. I can see it: green. I've been waiting to see something like that for so long. Look at it, it's green.

'Why not go to it?' said a sitter.

'I can't. I've not strength to go anywhere. Water, there's enough water to swim in. I can hear music. I can hear it. Where is it?

Somewhere somebody is playing. It is like an orchestra. I seem to know the theme very well, but I cannot quite recognise it. I can't have forgotten it. Where is it? It's gone. Let me hear it. Oh, don't torture me; let me hear it; give me music.'

The musician grew quite excited again, and a Debussy record was put on the gramophone. 'What is that noise?' he said. 'Oh, a record.' He listened and named the composer and the piece. But before the record ended, he said: 'I don't want to listen to any more. I can't take too much just yet.' After a moment, he said: 'I want to go down to the valley. I see the valley. I see someone beckoning to me. I'm free. I'm free.'

He seemed to be slipping easily away when, unfortunately, a sitter coughed. He was startled out of control, and then P'shanta spoke.

'What a pity: when he was just getting away. Poor young man. He has suffered so much. Bring near those who know him, so that he can see them.'

P'shanta then addressed the musician: 'Go now to the valley of soft music. See where your friends await you: the musicians. Listen to their names as they are read. See, there is one who knows you. He opens wide his arms: a teacher probably. You will sleep now for a long time, and then awaken to greater happiness than you ever dreamed of.'

P'shanta turned to the sitters: 'That is a good piece of work done. We will let you know how he gets on. Perhaps he will come himself, but that won't be for a long time.'

The Dead Poet

I well can see the splendour of a sun
And feel its warmth from rays outflung
And hear the music of a thousand masters
Blend into one
Bathe in swift waters; drink the cooling dews
Of countless blossoms gay with lovely hues
Cry from my heart's great gladness unafraid
Joy to diffuse.
From friendship's golden cup I freely sip
Feel wisdom's kiss fall chastely on my lip
Still know that life's great wonder book is mine
In which to dip.
Yet in their quiet grief they cried
'He died!'

Patrick, a casualty of the First World War, gives an account of his death

Think of us all as youths aspiring to things we felt were going to be beneficial to people. We felt able to face any difficulty, possibly because hardship had never touched us, for we had been guarded from infancy by kindness, surrounded by things that most people lack.

We knew most certainly that there were others who could not taste of the good things, who lacked much of the comfort that is, after all, a necessity; that there were many who had not had the opportunity of being properly educated. We tried to reason why some should come into their kingdom and others be veritable beggars at the door, and we resolved so to change things that all might share in the richness that this world can provide.

Then came the tragic experience of the war in which we served. One by one my friends were killed. It was my lot to receive the news of their going, one by one, sometimes in twos, and to go through the experience of seeing a whole company go, leaving perhaps one or two behind.

When my time came to go into another world, I had reached the stage of becoming the complete cynic. I wanted to die, not because I thought that in some far heaven, I would be far away from all that disturbs, but because I had seen my dreams shattered; because I had seen those whom I loved gone, as I thought, for ever; because I had seen their noble endeavours turned to naught.

Many times, I would say to myself: 'But it cannot be. They were too glorious; they lived too well for that. Surely somewhere I will find them again.' But then the stress of circumstances would overcome me, and I would become numb with distaste of the troubled conditions in which I lived.

Remember, this was not self-pity, but because the whole of humanity seemed to be rushing on its doom. I felt that there was no management in the whole of creation, that men were but puppets in a show, dancing to the strings of malevolent influences.

'Why should I', I questioned, 'with no desire to live, I who feel that nothing matters any more, why should I be the last left here? I know it is because there is still further torment for me to suffer.'

Then death came. What happened? Just what I expected might happen. I lived, but I was not happy. I was still a cynic. It is a strange thing that when you are withdrawn from fleshy things, for a time, you insist, if you are so minded, that all that transpires is just dreams or fancies or visions. Very often it seems like that until the reality is well established and you begin to react to your environment like a babe struggling with its limbs and with its lungs in unaccustomed air.

Many came and spoke to me, but I would have none of them. I was not sure that I was pleased to be living still. Oblivion would have been preferable. But occasionally, as it does to every soul, the real part of me persisted in coming upwards and dominating the situation.

My friends have told me that they were very much in despair about me, and tried various things to awaken my interest in my surroundings and in themselves, but that I was so very unapproachable that they often wept at their inability to give me any help whatever.

But there was one who persisted, and who, through time, made me realise that I was indeed in a world apart from this earth. He said to me: 'I think it is pretty abominable of you to behave in this way. True, you have gone through some pretty ghastly experiences, but man, you are alive and there is life waiting for you, beckoning you. Buck up and look around you. We are wanting you; others are wanting you. Be yourself and forget, and in time you will be able to see the reason for the experiences through which you have passed.'

I said: 'Well, I don't know whether you are even real or not. I have been through so much. I am dead, I know it. I remember dying, but I am not sure that I can understand what is happening to me now. As you say, I sometimes feel I want to live, and I find the youthful periods coming back and drawing me back into them. I am beginning to feel that I want to find again my ideals.'

'That is as it should be,' said my friend, 'but come with me and I will take you to see somebody who will cause something so amazing to happen to you that you will begin to wonder how you could ever have let yourself drift into a state like this.'

I went with my friend to where there were a great many people, all together, listening to the words that someone was speaking. What these words were, I cannot now remember, but I experienced the most extraordinary thing.

Sitting on the very edge of the crowd, I suddenly felt engulfed as if by warm sunshine from the speaker, sunshine that was so very welcome after the coldness of my former state. I felt a little bemused, a little bewildered, as though I would sleep and rest and find peace. The words meant nothing to me, it was the speaker, it was the atmosphere from him that sent the glow round me, and I did fall into a state of...shall I call it, unconsciousness, or sleep? And when I awakened, I was alone for a little while.

Then my friend came and said: 'Now, do you feel better after that experience?'

'I do not know.' I said. 'It might be yet another dream, but I feel the better for it and feel strangely warm and satisfied, and life is creeping back. Tell me more of this person.'

My friend unfolded to me a wonderful tale. I wish I could tell it to you, that tale of him who spoke and was able, through the very power of his own being to infuse others with the desire to live. You know who that person is: P'shanta, whom you did not know in those years, and whom even Mrs Thomson did not know. He had reached that stage of development where he was able to help me in my hour of need, without having spoken one word to me.

'Is it possible,' I asked, 'that I might speak to him alone?'

'I think so,' said my friend. 'It depends upon yourself. Let us try.' And forthwith, he went.

What happened next can only be understood by those who have personally experienced it. Coming face to face with one who lived on this earth, one who had not benefited by our vaunted civilisation and modern education, one who had not been adorned in fine raiment, talking with him was my first insight into the reality of the world in which I now live.

The dreams of youth, he told me, were still real. A man might gain his kingdom and not lose his soul. He might enter into the life he had to live and still not only dream, but fulfil those dreams.

I was privileged to become a disciple of that teacher. When he talked to me, I realised that I had found balm for my need. When I asked why certain things happened on this earth, the answer came so simply and so beautifully.

'The despair that you cast yourself into, my son, is only because you do not see the glory beyond yourself. Your lack of courage is because you are conceited, because you do not realise that beyond you is the source of all courage. You cry out because you think that you have lost the power to become wise. This is because you never were wise; because you have never begun to understand that within yourself is the source of all true wisdom. You were battered by a set of circumstances over which you personally had no control, and yet I say to you, my son, that you had within you the knowledge of what you were capable, even the storm of war and the awfulness of your experiences would have burnished you the brighter.'

How would you have reacted to reasoning like that? Have you felt the personality of one who can teach you to sublimate? Have you felt the power of one who can bring peace and calmness where only chaos was?

One day this friend said to me: 'My son, there have come to me others like yourself. I have had a purpose in gathering around me those who have gone through experiences like yours. In time you will learn that all of us are swayed by a greater influence than any man knows. The time is not yet ripe, but are you prepared to come back with me into the world in which you once lived, to mingle again with those on earth? Probably you will speak with those you have never known, and be denied the pleasure and privilege of speaking with those you have known. Will you come with me and help to bring about something of what you have dreamed?'

'My friend and teacher,' I said, 'if you say it, it must be. But how can anyone alter the state of the world? How can anyone break down the barriers that surround them there? How can anyone who has not seen the glory perceive it through mortal eyes?'

Do you see by that how my attitude has changed? I had decided, wrongly again, that it was impossible to experience on earth any of the joy which is the complete answer to those who doubt the reality of spirit living?

Again, I had to be taught many things, taken through many paths, made to understand how small and incomplete I was, to realise that the dreams of my youth could still come into being, through myself, no, but through others who, like me, were willing to learn the lesson that self means very little, that to gain the true soul, man must sink himself in others. True service is a hard lesson to learn, even here.

I had to take upon myself the harness; I had to desire to wear the cloak of servitude and to glory in it; I had to renew my youth and find that ideals never die; I had to learn that if a man looks for something he will find it. I had to realise the smallness and puniness of myself and to view the vastness of the whole with a different understanding.

What have I found through my service? I have found happiness and comradeship. I have joined my very much-loved friends. I am able to see in them, unspoiled, the beauty that was always there. I have added to myself new friends and I have found a joy that nothing can ever shake.

I pray God that I may in my own small way so serve that I may render service to him who so served me, and in so doing, return my thanks to the Almighty Father, the Spirit, the Source of all life.

The day of our transition is a very little thing: an experience that one soon forgets amid the billowing loveliness of life that actively engages one in the joyousness of the moment. But most people, if their thoughts turn before death in that direction, perhaps through the loss of one near and dear, make in their hearts some picture, some ideal of the heaven to which their own particular friend or loved one has gone. Most people, of course, waive the necessity of trying to picture themselves as dead, because to most people, death is a stilling of activity.

The possibility, not only of survival, in which I suppose most people believe, but of communicating with the dead, affects people very differently, and I, myself, can well remember hearing of cases on record and what transpired at an attempt to get in touch with those gone before. To me, it seemed all very puny and small, and very often I reviewed it with a certain sense of distaste and dislike.

Those of us who have died (those of us who now live) realise, of course, as all people who make foolish mistakes do, how absurd was our reasoning. There is, however, no way of comprehending the fullness of it until you are indeed embraced by it.

Many of us in youth were filled with the importance of ourselves and our own desires, not realising that adolescence lasts for longer than one is given to suspect, and that the struggle with life within bears the mark of its growing pains for a long period.

One does realise that at all times life is trying to gain supremacy, and that one is continually trying to find the path that best fits the ideals of the moment. All people are given to inspiration and aspiration, and all aspire to the best and the highest within them. I am perfectly sure that there is not one soul who has not, at some given moment, desired that the very best of him might be in evidence.

It has been my duty sometimes to scold those who would weep at what they thought was the loss of those who in their youth were cut off. I suppose it is the impossibility of really realising that youth, which is always so joyous and able to accept changes so easily, is uncrushable and unkillable and has a power within itself to right itself in due season.

In the responsibility one places upon life, and the duty one feels to one's kin and friends, there is always, I suppose, a sadness (very definitely so with most); and I know that to me there were moments when life seemed of the most supreme importance, when life held the acme of joy and perfection: when even the budding of a tree and the blossoming of a flower could give me what I felt to be the most supreme joy.

There have been moments when despair has gnawed at the very vital parts; when life seemed to be a mocking waste; when all else seemed to be cowering and unstable; and no one, least of all myself, had the power to shake up the conditions and reascend the throne of youth.

You have all felt that, I suppose, as you have all felt the annoyance of not being free to express yourself as you felt best. You have all known, no doubt, the agony with which you have faced failure after you had assured yourself that it was impossible to fail. You have no doubt found that you were unable, at a given moment, to be as strong as you thought you were, and you have reacted differently to those many sensations in your life.

The greatest trial of all, no doubt, has come to most of you: that of letting somebody go, who has meant nearly all of life to you. You have reacted differently to that too, and through the understanding that life, life beyond death, can be interpreted to suit the individual, you have found new joy: a new awakening.

We, who speak to you, we, who in our efforts have done what we can to bring those nearer to you whom you love, have been inspired by our knowledge of the need within ourselves. Making the discovery at first is always a very exciting thing: that one is not cut off in silence from the physical world and the joyous memory of it, but can still be an active participant in it.

To those newly gone, this is always very welcome and reassuring, because you know life beyond this immediate life requires some time for one to completely adjust oneself to; and all that one had ever regretted becomes magnified and immense.

One can always see without any shadow of doubt, if one is so inclined, that the love that one has given has never been enough, that the friends who have given so much, have not always been given the completeness that they deserve.

One can see that opportunities have not been made use of in the way they should, and one wishes one had the chance to live life over again, differently. This is almost always one of the first reactions. But it matters very little, because deep down in the soul of one remains a very strong residue of all that has ever been; and life, that is undoubtedly our supreme teacher, intends that we should benefit by our mistakes here, and there is a very definite impression left of earth life and all things that one has done or left undone.

There is no deceiving yourself or trying to quiet the pricking of your conscience. No smoothing over of something that you feel could well be excused. It simply does not happen. You see with a new clarity. You do not deceive yourself. If you are in despair and are bemoaning your own fate, your own littleness, it is only until you realise intimately that there is still an ever-increasing opportunity.

What wonderful solace that brings: to realise that the smallness of life, the long littleness of it, means nothing. That the beginning is at hand, and the will to live, and to do, and to be, and to accomplish all that one ever desired, is still strong. That is more marvellous than ever you could possibly imagine until you experience it.

Life deals out different ways to most people, and in the humbleness of living and in the simplicity of life one finds the nicest and the best. Wherever one goes, whatever part of the community one may seek to enter, whether it is the lowest or the highest, it is the simple things and the lovely things, the things that give joy, that make one replete with the fullness of life. In spirit living, one finds that out.

At first, my friends, there is after death the hesitancy of being afraid to embrace it, and there is a waiting, an undecidedness and a fear, because life has never dealt so generously with you before. You may feel that you have already learned all there is to learn about life, and there is nothing more. That you have already been to highest and lowest points. That feeling will remain until you learn the spiritual part of your life: and once you understand the true meaning of living, there will be no desire to retrace one's steps.

Living spiritually is living with the intensity of one's whole being, and being pious is usually being a hypocrite. The two are quite distinct, and one cannot put on a cloak of piety in the Spirit World. It deceives no one. You are known for what you are, for what you radiate about you, and for what you do.

I think during this time, when there is so much that seems only to lead towards destruction, that it is well if we can strike that note and assure you that, whether you die or live, whether you see kingdoms destroyed and reborn, whether you feel that all you have held sacred and loved can be at any moment destroyed, it is well to know this: that good and all these things of the spiritual kingdom are indestructible, and that even in your own heart, within your soul, you have by your own creating, formed something that cannot be destroyed.

One must give oneself to the Creator. I am glad that I lived because I loved it. I had much joyousness. I had the fondness of parents and of many friends. I had experiences of travel and meetings with all kinds of people, and it gave me in my short life, a fullness of living. But I too thought that life could give so much more.

Now, in a different way of living, I still have friends. I still have the joyousness of those I love. I have made new friends, and very dear they have become to me. I have found with many different people new experiences that have taught me something, and I have from this very earth learned new experiences that have passed me by before.

I have learned all the time, and I have joyed in my learning. I am able to place myself in line with those who have found the fount whence all wisdom and life comes: and I, with countless others, have learned that to serve another, without thought of self, is indeed the true way to serve oneself. I know, as others do, that come what may, God's Kingdom stands and remains indestructible. The war, and talking of war, can never harm the soul that is secure in its own spiritual outlook.

I am glad that I am able to pass that message on to you. Let us, those in the flesh and those without it, do our best, through the spirit that moves in us, to play our part to reconstruct the ideals of living, and do our best to foster in all men (our neighbours and our brothers) an ideal for spiritual living.

Richard, an airman and casualty of the Second World War, gives an account of his death

I don't remember dying. How difficult it is to think oneself into a condition which has no true relationship with what one feels. Death used to mean decay, and dying, decrepitude. Only in the circumstances of war did one begin to think of the suddenness of death in life.

There is no pain in dying. To me there was the swift thrill of fear, and the fear of the unknown can be terrifying. No doubt fear numbed my physical sensations. I wonder if that were so, or whether my other self, knowing what was inevitable, guided my body to its destruction. I remember shutting my eyes very tightly just before the impact so that the blinding flash I saw...what was it? The explosion of a shell that held me to my other self? I daresay that by listening closely one would hear the explosion from eggshells as birds were hatched.

I seem to digress. Let me say then that apart from the prelude to it, I know nothing of dying. Yet I never lost the consciousness of it. After the explosion I felt so isolated and alone. And there was a great stillness.

As time goes, it probably lasted a few seconds. Then the great silence ended and motion began. I rocked to and fro, increasing in momentum. I felt faint and nauseated by it. How odd to say those words! They seem slightly ridiculous now, but the sensation was real.

As the rocking movement slowed, I seemed to focus my attention upon a disc of light, dull at first, rather like a pale moon, and the motioning sensation slowed towards stillness. The disc of light grew brighter and still more bright, till I felt it would blind me. Suddenly it dissolved itself, and there was a great clarity, so clear and so pure, I can compare it to nothing I have ever experienced.

Now I felt lighter than air, buoyant and conscious of myself suddenly as a unit. I seemed to draw within myself a great draught of air, much as a new-born baby does, I expect. I could feel myself steadying up and reaching out towards reality.

Now the great stillness moved. I became conscious of sound, undefined but certain. Then my eyes caught the light and reflected back images: and quickly as thought travels, I knew I was whole and in one piece. Though alone, I had no fear, and could have remained within the circle of sensation for ever quite happily.

Suddenly I became aware of someone dressed in white from head to foot. I turned towards him. He was a stranger to me. He wore a band of living blue around his forehead, and his whole being was resplendent. I was at peace with him. The beauty of his voice when he spoke, thrilled me. He said with a smile: 'You trust me. That is enough. Come with me.'

As he turned to go, I to follow him, he lifted his hand to touch my forehead. At his touch, sensation leapt to a great climax with me, and there, right in front of me, tumbling over themselves in their excitement, were Peter and Tony and Jock and all the rest. Oh! The joy of their grinning faces, of a strong handclasp, and a thumb turned back, and the shouting and roaring, just as it used to be.

1940: Peter, a young airman, describes his introduction to life in the Spirit World

I was steering a fair course, rather high, when I came to grips with one of the opposite camps. The moment came quickly. I felt myself descending with great force. I thought I was sinking into unconsciousness, but actually I was falling through the air as well. I felt great pain. Everything became darker and darker, until it became altogether black. Then a pinpoint of light whirled all round me. Everything I had ever done, or, witnessed, seemed to move round me at terrific speed. It was like a bad dream.

Then I saw new faces, especially of fellows, who, I knew had gone out. I was afraid and wondered what had happened to me. I did not realise I had gone out. I thought it was all fantastic dreaming. I wanted to say: 'Hello, Bill! Hello, Ted!', but I seemed tongue-tied.

As I became conscious (that is, as the dreaming and the whirling all about me stopped), I saw a lady beside me. I thought I was in hospital. I felt my head bound, and something cooling put to my lips. Then there were restful arms beneath me, and I tried to raise myself, but I was too weak, as if all the blood had been drained from my body. I fell asleep and when I came to, I really was in hospital.

I was soon fit and strong and then I was told what had happened. I had never thought of dying. I had expected to come back with the rest and see the jolly old times return. On earth, we don't give enough thought to what is in front of us. If we understood more, we'd be better able to stand up to things. We would know that there is no need to fear death.

The moment I realised that I was really dead, an overpowering fear set in. We've been taught to fear death. Like so many others, I had smiled tolerantly at the teaching of the churches, but now I wondered what might be going to happen to me. But there are so many good people here to minister to us: ordinary people, not angels, tend you and help you, just as on earth.

I never knew my grandparents on earth, and none of my immediate family is dead, but those who were caring for me went to no end of trouble to find my relations. Some I'd heard of, and some I'd never heard of.

The Spirit World is very like the one I've left. I go about and see people, and now that I'm not afraid, I speak to them and note the strange things about me. I have received kindness, and been healed and made aware of a real world. I know too that it is possible, when I understand the laws, to go back to those I have left and affect them and put into their minds the consciousness of my safety and well-being.

It's good to know that I am still alive and can do a hard day's graft. I have still in my heart desires that I can talk about now, for I am no longer afraid of people laughing. One or two of my new friends actually seem to know of my innermost desires.

I am told that my time to speak is drawing to a close. How I came here, I don't know. I know that none of you can see me, and so it's easier to speak. While I am here, I know that I'll be taken care of, and that I'll be able to go away safely, rejoicing in the opportunity given me. I have found true billet and am safe and sound after hazards. I have recognised friends and relatives, and have found a new sphere of service for which I shall soon begin to prepare.

And now I appeal to you. Why be afraid to tell all you know, so that people like myself may share your knowledge and be prepared to face all eventualities? Let the young folk realise that religion can be real without sanctimony. Let them live freely and joyfully. I know now that life conquers death.

1942: Peter returns to speak to the sitters

It came as a shock to realise I was dead. It is so surprisingly easy to live, and the thought that death was over, was difficult to assess. There was nothing in dying. I did not feel it. When I realised that I was alive, it was like putting the reverse into action.

The excitement of seeing new things and of meeting people didn't leave me much time to come to grips with myself. I took what came, grateful to the people who helped me. I was sorry I was dead, and felt it was hard lines to be out of things so soon. But there were plenty of compensations. A lot of fellows came across and I made myself busy hitching them up, and forming a group. This idea helped us to settle more quickly.

Most of my relations are still on earth, and those who are dead, I didn't know. I got to know them in time, but I found it easier to get on with people I knew on earth. The others seemed superior a little. When I was with them, I felt like a child with elders, and was shy of using all the opportunities I had of making friends.

That idea has quite vanished now, but for a time I preferred to be with the boys, exchanging views. Our complaint was of being out of the show. We were not a curious bunch, and time hung heavy on our hands. Some of us got lost at times, and we found that they were back with their squadron, and miserable.

I was eager to do something to help the squadron too, but I quickly got into a mess and realised that there must be an art in helping those on earth. So, I applied to those who seemed to know about these things, with excellent results. I go back to the squadron now and like it, though the personnel have changed since I was part of it.

Home is still a sore point with me. I decided to refrain from going back, but a younger brother needed me, and I went more and more. That gave me the biggest heartache: to be so near, to see, to hear, to touch, and yet not to be heard. I had to learn how not to mind. I believe there is a way when one is schooled, and has learned the art, to direct them to make enquiry to communicate.

In my leisure moments, talking with other people (not my own crowd), I found how ignorant I was. There seemed to be an abyss between me and those who have been there for some time. I felt that the new way of living was a strange existence for one who was dead. I said to the boys: 'We know what's happened. We meet and discuss all sorts of things, yet we evade the important question. We're finished. We're alive but living differently. We're dead.'

Most of us hadn't thought of death. I hadn't, but I did think the dead differed from the living, not necessarily that they would have wings and a harp, but that they would be different from what they were on earth. I decided that I had better find out where I stood. Was this a temporary place? I began to enquire and watch, and saw that other people seemed to be happy and unconcerned about death.

It seemed curious that when we were alive, we were sent to school and had scripture lessons, and went to church and spoke the creed and were confirmed. That was an act to make one religiously prepared for life on earth and the hereafter. But it seemed to have no bearing at all on the life I am leading now.

I found that instead of being discountenanced because I had been careless concerning religious matters, it just didn't matter. Religion here just didn't seem to exist. But when I expressed this opinion, a friend took me round and showed me that all sorts of religious sects still existed. 'Is this not the end of that?' I asked. 'Is one not automatically good here? Is there not a stable religion for everyone? Are we in a transitory stage, no better than before?'

'It all depends on your point of view,' said the friend. 'You'll hear all sorts of doctrines. You must decide for yourself. But no one looks askance at you because you use your own mind.'

He told me to form my own opinions. I thought hard. Amongst those I met were people of different temperaments. They were certainly good. What was their religion? Church of England? Roman Catholic? Non-conformist: or, what?

When I asked them, they simply smiled a grown-up smile. Not many tried to help me out, and I thought that rather unkind. Later I realised that these people were all exceptionally good and broadminded. There was an absence of snobbishness and stiltedness about them. They were happy and friendly. I began to ask how long they had been dead, and I got some surprising answers. *If all these years pass and they are still here,* I thought, *heaven must be a long way off.*

I gave up worrying because I saw it did not get me anywhere. Religion, in any case, never had had a strong appeal to me. I had gone to church perfunctorily, and never taken it seriously. I decided now to enjoy myself.

Later I met my friend again, and he asked me how I was feeling about religion. I said I had decided I was not in heaven, but in some intermediate place where it was good to be. I was eager to live freely, like a bird, to feel exhilarated, to get rid of certain habits. I did not want to be religious. He asked me if I were being honest. 'That's the worst of you people,' I said, 'you seem to read thoughts. I was taught that after death I'd go to heaven and see God. I haven't. I'm shy of talking about it, but why is it? Is it just a matter of waiting? Some people have been here for hundreds of years. Do they lack righteousness?'

He said that many people expected to see God when they died: many religious people demanded it. He told me that if I used my senses, I'd discover how these excellent people I had met were content and happy in the life they were living, with a clear and excellent sense of God, without requiring to see Him. All life is a tangible part of God. The more I caught this sense of living and became part of it, the sooner I would feel the tangibility of a God so real, one ceased to expect a definite presence.

'Doesn't it prove that self-righteous people have no real assurance of God?' he said, 'when they are so insistent in their demands to see the personality of God? They have never the inner satisfaction. They have lost the great lesson religion should teach.'

This was rather difficult for me, but he told me to be happy and useful, to get a kick out of anything I could and I would soon find an answer to my problems. For a time, I felt myself at a loose end. I wanted to be told what to do, what the standards were. I felt there must be something I could do to fit myself for life in the new sense. I had a long time to live, so I did not wish to spend too long on idle speculation.

I was eager to learn for learning's sake, and I was not ashamed of it. There was no need to pretend I was not good at certain things. To be at one with things here, it is better to be truthful, for people see through conventional standards. It is disconcerting to find a person hearing what you're not intending to say. The people who took the trouble to let me know that there was no need to be conventionally bound, helped me a lot.

What are my conclusions?

It would be easier for us young people who are forced to die early if we had a better start and were given a better preparation for the new life. Some people are perfectly miserable at first. They won't understand the new way, and they suffer badly. It is not fair to keep death from young people and then plunge them into it. Fortunately, young people adapt themselves fairly quickly, but they become scathing critics of conditions on earth.

I've sworn, because of the help that's been given me and the new outlook on life I've received, and my knowledge that life is never stilled, to dedicate my life to the service of those who seek to educate people here on earth, especially those still young. We should make deaths a happy occasion. I should like young people to be eager to know life as it goes on from stage to stage.

Many people here live in different worlds of their own. I can't yet live in the same world as those who teach me, but I am eager to learn now. I'm not afraid of being called a swot. What is important to me is the new way of living, and the falsity of the old. I've a new body, better than the old. I can speed like an arrow. I can learn to understand people so well that I know what they are going to say. I'm not afraid of real happiness, of burying myself in the good earth and feeling near to God.

How much people have sinned against life, in preventing continued talking between those alive and those dead, so that we could still remain loved ones in the family circle!

Peter: Six Months Later

Peter returned six months later and told the sitters that he was no longer eager to be with his squadron. He had got into a jam there, and had had to be helped to get away. He described the therapeutic treatment he received: healing.

It's startling to find how everything here is in advance of earth, as if one suddenly found oneself in a state of advanced civilisation. The ease with which things are accomplished is fascinating. When they treated me, colours were used. I was enveloped in different colours, culminating in a gorgeous violet which was the final stage.

The whole process probably lasted a week: by earth standards, that is. It was so healing it was worth being ill just to go through it. The very cells of my body seemed to grow out of nothingness. It is nice to feel warm and whole and alive and in one's right mind, and to feel quietude enveloping one.

The healing properties of quiet are extraordinary. I wonder if people understand the efficacy of quiet, if they'd be helped as I was. Learning to be quiet is essential for growth. It is communing with the self. It is as invigorating as colour. It gives a feeling of cleanliness. It gave me strength and finished the healing process.

The old energy returned to me, but with a difference. I felt I wanted to be good, but not good in the old way. 'Good' now means to me feeling the full virtue of well-being, wanting to fashion something perfectly, to do something well, to find an outlet in things too personal to speak of. When the period of quiet passed, I entered the field of activity again. Mistakes make one cautious, and I thought it better to admit ignorance and seek advice.

It is wonderful how things fall into line, and friends come along. People help so eagerly if, for instance, you get tired. That only happens if you fall into old habits and get too near physical people. Then you feel as if you were flying and short of oxygen. You get lightheaded and sleepy, but you soon learn not to do these things.

I have never been in trouble without finding someone at my side to help; and whenever you are eager to do something in the right spirit, someone leads you, and by watching him you learn how to do it. It is amazing how quickly you learn in the new conditions.

Aspects of life here are very like those on earth, yet very different. You can travel at a rate unheard of. It is thrilling to find yourself going a tremendous distance with the ease of breathing. At first, I did it without knowing. I used to say to myself: *How did I get here?* Then with thinking about it, I lost the power to do it and had to use the same old method of locomotion again, till, forgetting the process, I found the new power restored. The old physical body can only move by physical processes. When we use a finer body, the difficult ways of moving become altered.

In this world there are, as it were, six sides to everything. Everything is spacious. There is room to live, to move, to breathe and to express your will. You're not cluttered with people who put up signposts to direct you to their own straight and narrow way. When I came here, I was picked up by someone who treated me on my own level. 'Here are friends,' he said. 'There are lots of things doing. Make the best of it.'

They arrange things very cleverly. You are welcomed to the bosom of the family. When you are thoroughly rested and have had a look round, you find a little job to do: shall we say, weeding the cabbage patch? They take you for granted and offer you real friendship. You are anxious to emulate them and you soon become one of them.

My greatest inspiration has come from the friendliness and love of those who helped me to pick up the pieces and face the new life, unafraid. No thanks are expected here, only doing, creating. By living truly and freely, I'm giving something back to those who have helped me. I strive to be fitted to do as they do.

I'll make many mistakes, but however many I make, I need not be afraid to go back. Forgiveness is there without asking. Someone is ready to set you on your feet again, and chaff you on your mistakes without recrimination. They accept you as one of themselves. If you feel offended here by anything, it is only because you do not understand, and think yourself superior.

If I have any regret, it's that I had to leave the earth so soon. But would I have been able to appreciate it? If only I and others could come back and live out all we've learned. People lose so much by not knowing.

Peter: May, 1944

I've been learning fast. I used to feel like a new boy at school. Everyone seemed so superior. But I can be companionable now, and make friends with all sorts of people. We get to know our life gradually, and settle to the ordinariness of it: but it's not really ordinary at all.

When I lived on earth, I did not feel at all comfortable at the thought of life after death. Ideas of heaven seemed so cold. I felt there would be a 'drawing-room' atmosphere. I'd have to take off my boots, so to speak. But being alive after death takes your breath away. Instead of heaven, you find a 'cottage' atmosphere, with log fires and easy lounge chairs and dogs. We like to get together and create the atmosphere of the mess or the study at school, with no one to bother us. Then homesickness for earth completely goes.

Though life in the two spheres is at times indivisible, at others it is absolutely separate. We can shut the door between the two and forget there has ever been an earth.

I have enquired if there has ever been an account of our way of life here, and have been told that people on earth are averse to the ordinariness of it. Their minds are so cluttered with thoughts of heaven, that many people communicating, are forced, against their own wishes, to be dressed up with the ideas of those who put forth descriptions of how we live. I felt very angry when I heard this, and had such a desire to rush in and describe everything as it is.

I'm an apprentice now, although no one says so. I'm allowed to use my own initiative. I learned quite easily not to be a lone wolf, but part of a crew in organised control. Curbing my activities has taught me a lot. I don't so much now regret earth experiences. I've missed a lot, which would have added to my growth, and which I must learn some other way.

My greatest regret is that I have not left part of myself behind me. That's something I've been robbed of for all time. I'll have to learn to transmute that regret into something created, to stand a testimony to me.

Peter: October, 1945

I used to be rather nonplussed when people didn't seem to remember I was new, but treated me as their coeval. When I saw a group of people, I would draw near to hear their conversation and join in it. That sounds rude, but somehow it didn't seem so. I was surprised to find that everyone was tremendously interested in the war, and looking forward to the peace and the building of new conditions.

Most people are staggered at first by the naturalness of living here. In one way it is very ordinary, yet in another, it is anything but ordinary. The atmosphere is different. There is easy intercourse between people, and after a while, you never stop to think who anyone is. You know they'll accept you. Age doesn't matter much. You feel veneration for age: I mean for those who have been living here for many years. But they don't expect young people to feel awed in front of them.

I thought that there must be many interesting people I'd like to see, for the generations are not so widely separated as you might think. Interesting people who lived quite a few centuries before are quite accessible. When I first wanted to go and see certain people, I was told: 'Oh, yes, you'll be welcome, if you go about it in the right way.' I set out once or twice, but I hadn't the courage to go on. When I went with someone else, I felt shy, and waited to be spoken to, but I never was. You must be part of things here. If you're diffident, and don't feel able to hold your own with people, you might as well not be in their company at all.

You'd expect those people who lived on earth so long ago to be a little aloof, on their dignity. I haven't found them so. They're very questioning. You expect them to know everything, and then suddenly they dart a question at you about a very simple thing. I remember talking with one such person, and before I knew where I was, I was telling *him*, and he seemed very interested. Once you lose self-consciousness here, you begin to get on, to live.

A lot of the fellows were eager to be with their former associates in their own squadron. They felt they must be on the job. That no longer appeals to me. Sometimes I go back inadvertently, but find myself critical and out of tune. I don't belong. Yet others get quite a thrill out of it. My thrill was making new discoveries, meeting new people and trying to understand their perfected system of living.

There is here perfect order, perfect rhythm. The light is better and colours are more beautiful. Music, too, is the same as on earth, yet extraordinarily different. Besides performed music, there is music of a different order, which you have to be in tune with to hear.

Peter: February, 1947

My friends and I form quite a colony here. We've got a hangar, a magnificent hangar, and it's our meeting place: our club. We're still very proud of our squadrons. Can you imagine us then, a group of rough and tumble young men talking endlessly together? We're still politically minded and have many fierce arguments, and make judgements, probably bad, on the state of ourselves and world affairs.

Sometimes we feel superior to our fellows on earth, as if we've been promoted. At first it was: why should this happen to me? I'd so much to live for. Now we begin to crow a bit, and feel we've the best of it. But we've learned, by the smile of some older friend, to know when we're getting a little ahead of ourselves.

Our betters don't keep us under their thumbs. They treat us as equals. People who have been here many, many years and who are infinitely our superiors, listen to us and encourage us to express our ideas. We are gradually learning that the only way to grow is by trying to do things and not being afraid of making mistakes. So, here we are, with so much still to learn and experience, enjoying the privilege of equal intercourse with anybody we can justifiably talk with.

I used to wonder how long it would take me to get the nerve to contact certain people. This depends on one's own attitude. If you feel unequal or ashamed to approach someone, you cannot do so. Sometimes we invite someone to lecture to us at the hangar. Whichever of us has most courage makes the advances, perhaps to our favourite poet, or author, or hero. What a choice there is! Nobody ever refuses us if we're really anxious to learn. And do they know!

In this hangar of ours, we can engage in anything we like. We have contests of all kinds. Our bodies are our bodies: though I know they have changed for you can't see me or touch me! This body keeps perfectly well, but I must take care of it. I get tired, if I am not careful, unutterably tired. But I can go instantly to sleep for as long as I care, without fear of interruption. I wake at the moment I fix, absolutely refreshed and bubbling over with the joy of living.

So, you can imagine two or three hundred of us meeting together, say weekly, learning from our elders, and pooling our experiences. Some of us have decided the line we'd like to take and are already training for it. We arrive at the choice by trial and error, but it is a serious business and we face it seriously.

The preparation is more extensive and personal than we could have possibly imagined. Others of our crowd have been kicking their heels for quite a while, never having got over their disappointment at being dead. Perhaps conditions at home on earth make it difficult for them; perhaps their background is poor; but sooner or later they will be drawn into something and become absorbed like the rest of us.

What is it that impels one to take a certain course? It can't be fate, unless by that we mean inner aspiration. It guided me to the group who adopted me almost from the start: scolded me, cajoled me, praised me, and left me feeling that there was more in me than ever I'd thought. And this acted as a spur.

There are people with a wise, kind goodness. You've only to look at them and you feel enfolded in a radiance as if you were being warmed by the sun: a radiance of warmth and love and beauty. You leave them walking on air, feeling it's wizard to be alive.

9

COMMUNICATION

P'shanta discusses the best conditions for good communication

The act of communication is not brought about without much planning and effort. The medium and sitters must meet in as relaxed an atmosphere as possible, friendly but not credulous. The communicator has to overcome the difficulty of entering into physical conditions which are now alien to him. To function comfortably in these conditions, he needs the help of experienced controls.

In communication we make shells: or masks. These are finely conceived and constructed, but we have neither the time nor the energy to make them visible. They hold the communicator so that he is kept 'on the floor' within the radius necessary to speak directly, and to make the sitter feel his actual presence.

Unfortunately, masks can't always be made, and without them, there can be no personal control, no direct communication, everything must be relayed. Relaying does not provide the conditions for intimate talk between friends, but good tabular evidence can be given that way. We never waste energy making masks for tabular evidence. They are made to give the communicator a sense of comfort and stability, for it is important that he should feel secure when so near the physical. Sometimes, as the mask fades, you may hear me say to him: 'No, you won't fall.'

In the ordinary trance sitting, the amount of ectoplasm used is amazing. We build from it a mask, the duplication of the medium, a half-way house into which the communicator enters and becomes amplified. It is a physical substance drawn from the medium, with only a little from the sitters. The better it is built, the better the communication. If it were more complete, it would be materialisation, for physical and mental mediumship are very close.

The medium is within this structure, and it encloses both the communicator and the control. The communicator fits nicely so that he is comfortable in a physical sense. This gives greater accuracy of communication, lessens the communicator's fear of approach, and lets me slip in unobserved.

Making the first link is often difficult, for communicators are not always aware the mask has been made for them, and they may be unwilling to enter it. Some become blind as they approach, although previously, they could see the sitters clearly, but when they are inside the structure they see again. The mask it used partly to protect, partly to reassure the communicator. It makes it easier for him to think.

Unfortunately, we can't make masks on every occasion. It depends on what we can gather from the sitter, and on his psychic and emotional responses. The mask is very delicate and may be rent at any moment. A slight disturbance, even some condition from the sitter, may destroy it. The mask is what makes the sitting successful. It is the living energy of the sitting.

The consciousness of the medium must be subdued. She is enveloped in a fine steam, like a tent around her. The steam condenses and grows thicker and thicker until nothing of the medium is seen at all by the communicator. In this cloud a light appears. This is the control. The light is vibrating rapidly, and becomes stronger and stronger, until the steam is negligible. I should add that neither the steam nor light are visible to the sitter.

When control is established, the conscious mind of the medium is subdued and the control combines with the brain power of the medium. There is a vast part of her mind left: the subconscious, or, superconscious as we prefer to call it. This is always active. The control merges his light with the superconscious of the medium, and with the fusing, you get a very much brighter light. Rays of electricity radiate in all directions.

Everything is now ready. A magnetic current is sent along. That is the communicator. Along the line are stationed at different points sentinels, each one a ray. The communicator touches one of these rays, preferably the strongest for him. The junction of the two magnetic forces sets in operation the process known as communication.

You get a fusion of minds. The communicator is now thinking, that is speaking, in his own field. He is giving information. The control is so close that speech comes right through. When the line is perfect, it comes automatically. The communicator operates and the control is not in evidence at all.

It is easy to see how a slight disturbance will upset perfect functioning along the line and give confused messages. A sudden question may destroy the structure; it breaks the flow of thought because the structure does not depend upon one mind alone.

The medium is in a telepathic state towards the control, but the sitter is also in a telepathic condition. Something in his mind may be opposing transmission and causing unsatisfactory communication. If he is dilettante in his attitude, so will his communications be. He is often the strongest point in the communication. Mind and mind, to meet perfectly, must be of the same vibration.

P'shanta discusses some of the main difficulties encountered when setting up the process of communication

Most people think that a communicator is only too eager to give information, but that is not always the case. Very often he is anxious, he feels he doesn't know how, he suffers from stage fright and is dumb when the moment is right. He may want to say only: 'How are you? I'm glad to see you. I'm happy.'

Other communicators think that if only they were left to themselves, they would do much better. 'Why is a medium necessary?' they ask. 'I want to do it myself.' Even if we allowed them to try it alone, they would forget most of what they wanted to say. I often have to extricate a shred of evidence from the jumble of a communicator's thoughts.

Others are overwhelmed by the joy of the moment; the human desire to be at one with their loved ones is so great that evidence is quite forgotten. They feel stupid when asked to introduce themselves, and often feel that 'Father' or 'Mother' should be enough. The last thing that would occur to them is that you could doubt them. Their individuality is so strong to themselves that they can't conceive of your not being able to recognise it. They cannot be cool, calm and collected.

We must, therefore, have people who prepare them psychologically for what we have to do. Until Julian (control) has spoken to the communicators and given them some idea of what is wanted, the links are not opened. Sometimes it is best just to let them be themselves. If it is soon after their passing, they may be incoherent, but speaking helps them, for they find they are not cut off from their friends after all.

Then Julian asks for little points of evidence, not obviously, but as if it were himself interested, for example: 'I don't know your name. What is it?' Usually, they give a full name as an introduction, so we say: 'William' instead of 'Bill' to the sitter. By dint of questioning in an interested way we get many evidential details. As the communicators realise what is required, they proffer these themselves and talk of things the sitters may have forgotten.

Julian acts as a medium between the communicator and myself. He acts for the communicator, and I, for him. If direct speech is possible between us, then everything is easy except when consonants run together so that I can't hear easily. The initial letter 'A' is difficult to me. This may cause distortion because I depend on hearing.

Sometimes I may have radioed to me what is said. The message may be incomplete, not coming quite through the barrier that prevents the control coming close. It prevents the impetus of sound waves, so that I may hear only every other word. I may get the rhythm, one beat and not the other. The words may or may not make sense, the gaps may or may not be filled.

Communication can bristle with difficulties for the uninitiated. I may say: 'I think this is your mother.' The sitter wonders why I have to say 'think', but the spirit does not just come and say: 'I am his mother.' She may be so excited, or so afraid that she loses all power of speech. I have to do it all for her. I have to sense the relationship and find a common link, until eagerness to communicate overcomes the difficulties. I may sense 'Mother', or 'Sister', but the communicator may actually be the Mother-in-Law or Aunt.

In transmission there is often a picturisation which I must interpret in words. This is why many things are said in different ways. The possibilities of mistakes are many; sometimes even the reverse of the thought is given.

We know by the reaction of the communicator if the thought has been correctly transmitted. If he becomes annoyed, we try again and again until he is satisfied, even if the sitter is not. I like to make a link where the communicator is able to speak as if he himself were actually transmitting.

We can never say: 'This will take place', or, 'This will be the result', for communication is dependent on conditions surrounding the individuals concerned. Even when prostrate with grief, some people are rigid and repudiate all efforts to reach them. In the initial experiences of communication, the attitude of the sitter is all-important.

People who expect a first sitting to be nothing but factual evidence forget the personality of the communicator. Communicating for the first time is a very tremulous business. Your dearest can be the last to speak because they are afraid their emotions will overwhelm them.

It is then that the tact and understanding of the operators comes in. They gauge the personality of the communicator and promote the condition requisite for communication. At first it is usually loving exchanges and there may be no factual evidence at all. If you want to study mediumship, you must realise there has to be a period of this.

Spirit people take great trouble to assess your environment, more than you think. Even if they don't actually see what you suffer and enjoy, they can assess your condition through their emotional powers. But they are not cognisant of all that you do and say. You must not assume that they know certain things, nor be disappointed if they do not know or cannot remember some particular thing.

We vary with the methods used in communication. It depends upon the communicator, whether or not, I am able to say what he wants to say. I may not understand his words, if, for example, he speaks in Gaelic, so I must understand what he wants to say. Sometimes Julian gets the idea and passes it telepathically to me. Then I say what I think Julian thinks the communicator wants to say.

It is seldom that a communicator comes armed with evidence. Indeed, we do not encourage that because such evidence is very difficult to convey. Spontaneous evidence comes if control is good.

Rupert discusses difficulties he has encountered as a control where sitters are concerned

Sitters are very important, especially in the early stages of development. They could so easily influence the medium towards things which have nothing to do with communication.

In Mrs Thomson's home circle, I had to fight down such things as ghost hunting. When a sitter's house was burgled, I had to ask if they wanted Mrs Thomson to be a bloodhound or a medium. Later I was asked to prove or disprove a certain medium. Then someone asked me to allow his father, in spirit, to deliver through the medium an address on temperance.

Some people assume that we agree with their pet theories, but we cannot allow any pronouncements on, for example, politics, to be made through the medium, though of course we all have our own views. Working as members of the group we cleave together for one purpose: truth.

The best sitter is often the new sitter who has not been influenced by reading and talking with other people. He exercises very little influence on the sitting because he has no preconceived ideas.

Most trouble is given by sitters with strong ideas of what they want and don't want. If they put questions persistently, we try to ignore these because they spoil the evidence. This resistance to the will of the sitter uses energy and so lessens our power of giving evidence. Suggestions coming telepathically from sitters are another great difficulty. We have to divert the sitter's thoughts and this demands much attention.

Ordinarily in communication there are far too many who want to speak, so elimination must take place. Choice is made of those most needful or most helpful. The sitter should not wish strongly for any one person for that spoils his evidence.

Raymond (control) discusses some of his early experiences in communicating

I had many interesting experiences communicating with my family. Sometimes these were merely funny; sometimes they might have been rather tragic. I learned a lot and took note of things, wondering if I could get anyone to help me. I decided to experiment to try to find the best method of communication.

With one trance medium, rather untrained, I was frightened by the grotesque motions she made, as if I myself were making jerks and gestures. I thought at first that I was to blame for it, and wanted to get out, not to upset her. I was very uncomfortable for I thought she might take a fit and I might be responsible for her death. Then I got into the link and actually got through two, or, three good bits of evidence.

I was interested in the mechanism of communication and studied it. Finally, I decided that the only way to be sure of an evidential contact was through the conveying of personality. It must be carefully done. To people who have experienced real personality, in close link, so that the medium is turned for the nonce into the communicator, it is most convincing to the sitter and most satisfactory to the communicator. Factual evidence comes better afterwards.

It is important to remember that communicators are out of their true element. They must become partly physical so that their memory is linked with the physical. That is why foreigners naturally revert to their mother tongue at first, no matter how expert they may be in English.

That too is why tests are very difficult. Communicators have agreed to say something after death: it doesn't come because they are not in their natural element and the conditions thwart it. But it may come unexpectedly if something links and the process unlocks itself.

The communicator must be able to align himself with the medium and the operators for good control. He must feel natural in communication. That is why, working in a band, we build a cavity, or mask, to isolate the communicator from upsetting conditions, so that he forgets them and feels as if he were in his natural element.

Depending on conditions, P'shanta can relay what is said and interpret what he feels the communicator wants to say; or he can bring him in so clearly that he merges with the other unit and becomes as exactly reproduced as possible. The communicator becomes the control. This is rare in mediumship because development is seldom continued long enough.

All our endeavour is to convey the individual characteristics of the communicator. When conditions are good, the communication will be of a personal nature, giving the gestures, idioms, voice and even features of the communicator. The personality, if conveyed in integrity, is better evidence than anything else.

Peter, the young airman, discusses his experiences with sitters

I used to think it would be quite easy to give evidence. I thought that I would be able to hit the target every time. I would only have to remember certain facts and pass them on. I did not at that time realise how many factors were at work in a sitting, or how much depends upon the sitter.

If the sitter is suspicious of the medium, then however delicately it may be hidden, the atmosphere is charged with suspicion. This has a stifling effect upon the communicator, as if he were wrapped in cotton wool and could scarcely breathe. Everything he meant to say goes; sometimes he can't even think of his own name. He has a sense of frustration, and gets impatient with those assisting, who in turn, are short with him.

The sitter meantime is probably tapping his pencil on his pad and thinking: 'This is just what I expected.' At the end, the communicator exhausted, feels: 'If that is communication, I'm finished. It doesn't get you anywhere.'

Sometimes in such a sitting, when I am trying all, I can sense that the atmosphere seems suddenly to change; there's a little more air to breathe, an opening in the cloud. Something I have said has struck a chord. I think: 'At last they know it is me!' But often the moment passes and things are as they were once more.

On one occasion, I undertook to help a friend who had the opportunity of communicating with his relatives. Knowing that the chief difficulty would be that when he entered the controlling point, the communicator would forget what he meant to say, I promised to stand by and help him. Together we prepared the evidence and rehearsed it thoroughly, so that it would be a completely satisfactory sitting.

The day arrived, and the communicator began to give his carefully prepared evidence, but was interrupted by a sitter saying: 'Do you remember such-and-such?', referring to an incident quite away from his train of thought. He lost control and turned to me with a baffled: 'What do I do now?'

I find such irrelevant questions very disconcerting. Imagine how you would feel if during a conversation at the tea-table someone suddenly said: 'What is your name?' Sometimes that question has been asked when I'm quite sure I've already given my name. It's not fair to switch suddenly from one topic to another.

My friends used to be particularly sceptical, but I've found that gullibility can build as great a barrier as scepticism. One of my friends in Spirit communicated with a relative who was a convinced Spiritualist. 'My dear boy,' said the relative, 'I know it's you. You don't need to give me any evidence. Tell me about your life and the world you're living in.'

She then proceeded to give my friend, at great length, her own ideas on the matter. Her views were not convincing. The communicator was bewildered and finally said to me: 'If that's what I'm doing and if that's the world I'm living in, the sooner I make for a lunatic asylum, the better!'

I have found that it is better to forget I am giving evidence, and to behave naturally. I have put together a code of rules:

1. Be as natural as possible;
2. Keep your head, your sense of humour and your temper; and
3. Take your time.

The rule for sitters should be: don't ask disconcerting questions!

A final warning by P'shanta to sitters

I object strongly to communications (no matter what channel they come through) which tend to weaken the individual and sap his strength for grappling with problems. I object to grand claims being made about the sitters' friends being concerned with work of great importance in the new life they function in. I object to pseudo-idealism which has no foundation, and which is only words that go mostly over the heads of the people that listen to them. I object to all theories coming through spirit channels that cannot be proven. People can indulge in their foolish fancies without spirits encouraging them. I object to the miraculous (under whatever auspices), knowing that the Laws of the Universe govern all things, and are not the special prerogative of the few.

It is very hurtful to me to be asked to substantiate communications which I know are only absurdities. It is my intention always to guide and direct you by practical common-sense methods only. All I have said until now, and all I will ever say, can be said to intelligent people and understood by them.

I have at all times, gently I think, tried to persuade people that the common-sense method is always the best when dealing with psychic things.

It is important that communications tend to prove the individuality of the communicator. The matter they contain takes second place. Spirit people have not in any way taken on the cloak of miracle worker, and you should receive guardedly all communications which suggest that they have.

Though your dear ones will always wish you the best in life, they cannot by direct means relieve you of your obligations, and it is foolish to ask them to do so. You should not ask them to prove their presence in a visual way, or to use physical means such as knocking. Channels, through which promises of such things come, are open to suspicion.

Do not be flattered by communications which attempt to decide your fate, either in the next world, or in this. You alone are the arbiter of your fate. Receive very sceptically any statements which promise you the development of wonderful gifts, or the help of guides. True, many guides are willing, but the channels are few.

Resent with every fibre of your being, the suggestion that you are not man or woman enough to face the ordinary happenings of life for yourself: and try to remember that people released from flesh are just as much concerned with their own living as ever. They must get strong, set their own house in order, and gradually understand the conditions, in which, and, through which, they are vibrating, before they can render you any real and practical service.

Sitters should be able to assure themselves that they are indeed communicating with their friends, and the attempt should never be undertaken lightly. But first and foremost, sitters should always remember, they are here on earth to live a human life.

10

A HUMAN LIFE

'We are here on earth to live a human life':
Mrs Thomson's human legacy

We can see from the selection of material we have used to write this book that Mrs Thomson was a conscientious medium, who provided great comfort through her work: but this was not all. She was also a human being who faced incredible challenges, yet managed to leave a legacy as a caring mother and grandmother: and this should also be recognised.

Life was difficult for Mrs Thomson, particularly as a child and young woman, yet, she faced the challenges, learned from them, and moved on.

She was born in England (Woolwich) on 7 June 1894, and was the daughter of Edward McCanlis (soldier in the Royal Artillery) and Mary Ellen Gee.

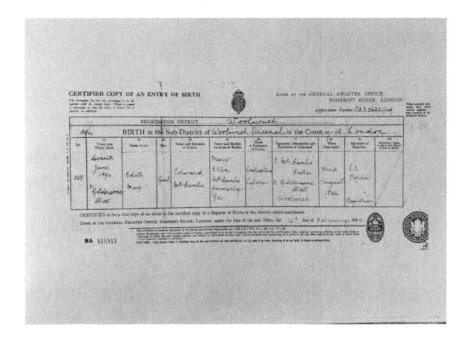

Mrs Thomson's birth certificate

Sadly, Mrs Thomson's mother died from nephritis (kidney inflammation) a few months after she was born.

Family circumstances were far from ideal. Her father, who was unemployed, was forced to live in a common lodging house, and Mrs Thomson was sent to live with her maternal grandmother. The situation was dire. Her father was described as 'nearly half starved', and her grandmother as 'very poor and aged and unable to look after Edith properly'.

The landlord and landlady of the lodging house eventually expressed their concerns to the Children's Aid Society. On 13 June 1903, when she was aged nine, Mrs Thomson was sent to live at the New Orphan House No 3, Ashley Downs, Bristol, and remained there until the age of seventeen, when she left to become a general servant at the home of a Mrs Ritchie in Essex. Not the most auspicious of beginnings, Mrs Thomson, nonetheless, refused to dwell on her misfortune: indeed, her family didn't learn about her life in the orphanage until 2020, when they first looked into the family tree.

New Orphan House No. 3 from the north, Bristol, c.1880.

Girls with balloons at New Orphan Houses, Bristol, c.1905.

Coronation celebrations at New Orphan Houses, Bristol, 1911.

In 1923, Mrs Thomson married John Thomson (*see below*), an iron turner, in Glasgow, and the pair went on to have two daughters: Gina and Jenny.

But it was the time of the Depression, and John was regularly out of work. For four years the family depended on unemployment benefit, and were forced to sell possessions. Fortunately, Mrs Thomson's domestic skills and knowledge of nutrition (learned as a general servant) enabled her to feed and nurture her girls into adulthood.

Gina (left) and Jenny (right)

During the Second World War (1939 - 1945), Mrs Thomson's health was poor. She was finding it difficult to combine her mediumship with the running of a home. Her doctor was concerned about her health, so it was decided that her daughter Gina, instead of joining the WAAF, should remain at home to help her. This meant Mrs Thomson could combine the duties of domesticity with the continued development of her trance mediumship, giving us the opportunity to understand more about life in the Spirit World.

Mrs Thomson had a very close relationship with both her daughters. When they were grown women, she would discuss psychology, philosophy and many other subjects relating to self-improvement with them: topics that sit well with the philosophy of Spiritualism.

Her knowledge and ability to give caring and useful advice, were no doubt a consequence of her many lifetime experiences; but probably the most important influence was P'shanta, her spirit guide.

We have already learned that Harriet McIndoe kept careful records of Mrs Thomson's trance sessions. These notes have served to introduce us to a host of lovely personalities in the Spirit World, and we should remember that each of these spirits once incarnated into a human body to learn about the many challenges encountered in a human life. But more than that: by going on to discuss their own development in the Spirit World, they have helped us to understand ourselves, and guide us on our own human journey.

First, P'shanta: Mrs Thomson's faithful guide. His wise philosophical words help us to understand what goes on in the Spirit World. Although highly evolved, he does not pretend to know everything, and when it comes to God, he says simply that the spirit of life in each of us is God.

Then there are the controls: Raymond, Julian, Rupert, David and Silver Pine (the healer). Each spirit is a different personality, and each strives to protect and assist P'shanta. They discuss the difficulties they face regarding the mechanics of mediumship from the perspective of the Spirit World, and it is evident, that self-improvement and progress are not limited to the physical world.

Finally, the selection of communicators who illustrate the naturalness (or, sometimes, the confusion) of death: the elderly man, the young musician, the dead poet, Patrick from the First World War and Richard and Peter from the Second World War.

The End of a Physical Life

When Mrs Thomson died on 17 July 1965, aged seventy-one, she left a positive legacy. Despite her materially impoverished beginnings, she remained mindful of her good fortune. From a spiritual perspective, she was able to shine on a journey that empowered the bereaved, giving them the knowledge that consciousness remains alive after physical death. This was particularly important during the period of heavy loss of life during the Second World War.

To balance that, she also had a supportive husband, two daughters and lovely grandchildren: and her love for them was well reciprocated.

In the words of Sheila (granddaughter), she was:

'...a very special lady, and it was an honour and privilege to have known her. She always greeted everyone with a smile, and made them feel so welcome. She was a wonderful, gentle and generous woman.'

Mrs Thomson and two of her grandchildren

THE GLASGOW ASSOCIATION OF SPIRITUALISTS

The Glasgow Association of Spiritualists admires the diligence of Mrs Thomson and her sitters. We thank Harriet McIndoe for her organisational skills and well-kept notes. We are humbly grateful for the participation of Mrs Thomson's guide, P'shanta, together with the controls and communicators, who came forward to address the sitters, providing them with good philosophy to help them on their journey of development in the physical world.

Through the words of all these people (incarnate and discarnate) we sincerely hope that you have learned and understood a little more about the philosophy of life both here, in the physical world, and in the Spirit World.

We must never forget that we are each an individual spirit on our own particular journey. Our spirit just happens to inhabit a physical body whilst in the physical world. We are responsible for our own actions in both worlds: and have free will to do as we choose.

The records compiled by Harriet McIndoe show that Mrs Thomson used her free will responsibly, and in the process, helped thousands of individuals, both in the physical world and the Spirit World. We must also remind ourselves that Mrs Thomson led a very challenging life as a child and young adult, which she appears to have handled with fortitude and dignity.

One wonders if this was why P'shanta chose Edith Thomson to disseminate his valuable philosophy.

Other Books by The Glasgow Association of Spiritualists

Stories of the Pioneers: Mediums, Healers and Psychical Researchers.
God to Malaria: Communications from the Spirit World.

Printed in Great Britain
by Amazon